£2.50

The Internet– Tweaks, Tips and Tricks

D1457802

Robert Penfold

Please note

Although every care has been taken with the production of this book to ensure that any projects, designs, modifications, and/or programs, etc., contained herewith, operate in a correct and safe manner and also that any components specified are normally available in Great Britain, the Publisher and Author do not accept responsibility in any way for the failure (including fault in design) of any projects, design, modification, or program to work correctly or to cause damage to any equipment that it may be connected to or used in conjunction with, or in respect of any other damage or injury that may be caused, nor do the Publishers accept responsibility in any way for the failure to obtain specified components.

Notice is also given that if any equipment that is still under warranty is modified in any way or used or connected with home-built equipment then that warranty may be void.

© 2010 BERNARD BABANI (publishing) LTD

First Published - August 2010

British Library Cataloguing in Publication Data
A catalogue record for this book is available from the British Library

ISBN   978 0 85934 721 1

Cover Design by Gregor Arthur
Printed and bound in Great Britain for Bernard Babani (publishing) Ltd

Computing used to be centred on business applications such as word processors and spreadsheets, and on home applications, which in practice usually meant games of one type or another. I suppose that to a large extent this remains the case, but the increasing use of the Internet, together with the power and sophistication of modern computers, has resulted in a fundamental change in the way computers are used. The importance of the Internet to individuals and businesses has steadily grown in recent years. Modern computing tends to be very Internet oriented. These days, being reasonably proficient at using the Internet is probably more important than knowing your way around the Windows operating system.

By any standards, the amount of information on the Internet is now truly staggering. There are literally billions of web pages, and some estimates put the figure at over one trillion (one million million) pages. Practically any information you require will be available on the Internet, but even with the aid of modern search engines it can be difficult to find the information you require. Using the Internet effectively is largely about finding the right pages without having to manually sort through literally thousands of pages that are almost right but not quite. This book shows you how to use search engines to find what you are looking for quickly and efficiently, without having to wade through thousands of irrelevant search results.

Unfortunately, the Internet is a slightly risky environment to operate in. There are web sites that try to infect computers with various types of malware, Emails that try to trick you into divulging passwords or personal information that could be useful to fraudsters, and a whole range of other deceptions and scams. If you start buying and selling online there are further deceptions and scams to watch out for. This book helps you to fully exploit the potential of the Internet while avoiding scams, computer infections, and other online hazards.

Many other subjects are covered, such as getting awkward web pages to display properly, finding free software to download, using the expanding range of Cloud computing services, using download managers to provide faster downloads, surfing privately, using the History facility to find a web site visited a few days earlier, etc.

A high level of computer expertise is not assumed, but readers do need to be familiar with the basics of using a PC running a modern version of Windows.

Robert Penfold

Trademarks

Contents

3

Downloading 33

4

eBay buying 51

5

eBay selling 63

6

Security 77

7

Browsers 93

8

Finding things 107

Cloud computing

What is cloud computing?

Cloud computing is a concept that has popped up from time-to-time since the early days of the Internet, but it is only in recent times that it has achieved significant popularity. Its dramatic increase in popularity is probably linked to the rise in popularity of netbook PCs and other portable computing gadgets. Most of these devices have quite basic specifications, and what by desktop computing standard is minimalist hardware. Cloud computing provides a way of reducing the burden on the computer's hardware, making it an attractive proposition for the users of the more basic portable computers. However, it would be wrong to regard cloud computing as strictly for users of low specification portable computers. In fact, if you use a PC it is virtually certain that you already do a certain amount of cloud computing. Cloud computing is where you use resources that are not located on your computer, or even on a local area network (LAN) to which it is connected. In the current context, the resources will be located on servers anywhere in the world, and in most cases you will have no idea of their location. They are of course, accessed via the Internet.

Probably most users undertake a certain amount of cloud computing without actually realising it. In fact many computer users do substantial amounts of cloud computing practically every day without realising it. Internet based Email systems are a common example of cloud computing. With these systems it is often possible to use an ordinary Email program to access your account, but most people do not bother to do things this way. Instead, they simply use the Email program that is included as part of the system. The exact way in which things are handled varies from one Email system to another, but you do not normally have an ordinary Windows program running on your PC. At most, some sort of applet will be run on your PC. To some extent the Email program will be running on the server of the service provider, and all your Email data will also be stored on this server rather than on your computer. In other words, the burden of data storage is transferred from your PC to the server, as to some extent is the running of the program. This is really just a variation on the system used in some large networks where there is a large and powerful mainframe computer and numerous "dumb" terminals.

An Internet search engine is perhaps the best example of extreme cloud computing, and it clearly demonstrates the way in which the power of a large computer can be accessed via the Internet. The user's PC has to do nothing more than send a few words of text to the search engine, and then display the pages of text that come back from it. This is good example of a PC operating as a "dumb" terminal in fact. The search engine does all the work using either a powerful mainframe computer and a huge database, or a huge network of smaller computers. This enables billions of web pages to be searched using massive computing power and database facilities, but the user needs nothing more than the most basic of PCs and an Internet connection.

Cloud services

Similar systems are used for many other online facilities, such as messaging systems, blogging sites, social networking, accessing and analysing financial data and online picture albums. With all of these it is a very convenient way of doing things, because the facilities are to a large extent Internet based anyway. In many cases you use your normal web browser to access the facilities, which appear to the user as just an ordinary part of the Internet. There is no need to download and install complex software and then link it to the appropriate Internet site, thus avoiding the complications that this often involves. It is now possible to take cloud computing beyond facilities that are already web oriented by using the services provided by Google, Microsoft, and others. For example, rather than installing a word processor on your computer and storing your documents on its hard disc drive, you can word process online. You use a program on the provider's server, which is also where you store your documents. Copies of the documents can also be stored on your computer, but this is optional. The range of cloud computing services is still quite limited compared to the huge range of ordinary PC software that is currently available, but most popular applications are catered for, together with some niche types.

Cost

An obvious attraction of cloud computing at the moment is that it is largely free. There is the cost of the Internet connection, but this is presumably something that practically every computer user would have anyway. Some cloud computing services do actually require the user to pay a subscription fee, but most types of cloud computing are free, and are presumably supported by advertising. It remains to be seen whether most cloud computing services remain free, or if eventually a subscription has to be paid for most of them. For the foreseeable future it seems likely that increased competition will keep most services free of charge. It also seems likely that there will be a steady increase in the range of cloud computing services on offer.

Drawbacks

Although there is much to be said in favour of cloud computing, it is not a case of "roses all the way". The main reason for cloud computing having consistently faltered until quite recently is probably a matter of connection speed. Most Internet users had ordinary dial-up connections until a few years ago. These have a maximum connection speed of just 56 kilobits per second, which in practice often turns out to be a speed of about 30 to 40 kilobits per second. Many users also experience problems with reliability. Cloud computing using this type of connection is not a very practical proposition. Everything can run very slowly even when relatively small amounts of data are being swapped between the main computer and the PC. An unreliable connection will waste more time and make it difficult to use the system effectively. A slow connection is impractical in situations where large amounts of data are being transferred, since the user might have to sit there waiting several minutes for the system to start responding again. Cloud computing really requires a good quality broadband Internet connection of some kind.

Cloud security

As malicious software and hacking are ever present threats on the Internet, security is obviously a concern when using cloud computing. Provided you take the normal safety precautions such as using a firewall and up-to-date antivirus software, there should be a minimal risk of anyone gaining access to your data by hacking into your netbook. There have been cases of large companies having their web sites hacked, but the data stored using online servers is almost certainly more secure than the data stored on your own PCs.

The right browser

It is not necessary to have a special browser for cloud computing, but that is not to say that any web browser can be used with any cloud computing facilities. Most cloud computing services are fairly easygoing, and will work with the majority of modern browser programs. However, it is advisable to check the requirements before trying to use any cloud computing services. Most of them will work perfectly well with the popular browsers such as Internet Explorer and Firefox, but it is as well to ensure that you are using a suitable program, and also an appropriate version of that program. If you normally use one of the less popular browsers it is definitely a good idea to check that it is compatible with any cloud computing services that you intend to use.

If problems occur even when using a suitable browser program, it is likely that one or more of the so-called browser plug-in programs are required in addition to the basic browser software. For example, it is sometimes necessary to have something like the Adobe Flash Player add-on installed. Most cloud computing services have a Help section that provides details of any add-on software that is needed, together with installation instructions. Browser add-ons are usually available as free downloads incidentally, so there should be no cost involved unless you have to pay for the Internet access while downloading the file. The typical file size is only a megabyte or two, so the download time should be extremely short. The lack of required add-on will often be detected by the facility you are trying to use, and automatic installation may then be offered. These automatic systems do not always operate flawlessly, but they are generally worth a try. Bear in mind that each of the popular web browser programs usually has its own version of the add-on software. If you are using the Linux operating system, check that the facilities you intend to use are compatible with this operating system.

Extra browser

Remember that it is not necessary to use the same web browser for everything. There is an easy solution if your normal web browser is not compatible with a cloud computing facility that you are eager to use. Simply install a web browser that is compatible with this facility, and then use it when you wish to use that facility. Your normal web browser can still be used for all other Internet related tasks. Provided your computer has a reasonable amount of memory installed there should be no problems if two different web browser programs are run simultaneously. You can then switch rapidly between surfing and cloud computing applications.

Word processing

Google Docs is probably the most popular cloud computing word processor, and in order to use it you must have an account with Google. A Google account provides access to a wide range of cloud computing facilities including Email, blogging and web site creation. Google Docs is actually a bit more than a word processor, since it also includes a

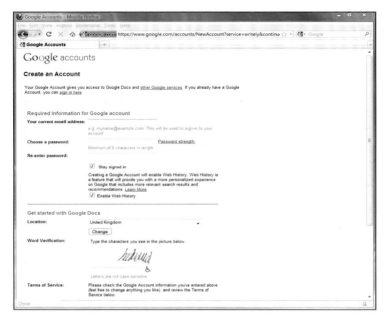

Fig.1.1 Use this page if you need to open a Google account

spreadsheet facility and a slideshow creator. Go to this web address to make a start with Google Docs:

http://docs.google.com

This will take you to the login page, and it is obviously just a matter of signing in if you already have a Google account. If not, operate the Get Started button and enter the necessary information on the new web page that appears (Figure 1.1). If the Google facilities will be used on a portable computer it is probably best not to use the "Stay signed in" option. Operate the "I accept Create my account" button once the form has been completed.

You can then sign into Google Docs, and the new screen will look something like Figure 1.2. I have already added three documents, which are listed in the main panel on the right. In order to open an existing document it is just a matter of left-clicking its entry in the list, and it will then be opened in a new tab. However, this panel will obviously be blank when starting from scratch, and a new document has to be created by operating the Create new button and selecting the Document option

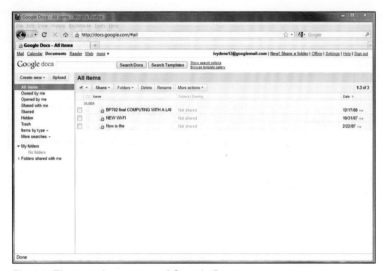

Fig.1.2 The opening screen of Google Docs

Fig.1.3 A blank word processor document in Google Docs

from the drop-down menu. This will produce a blank document in a new tab (Figure 1.3).

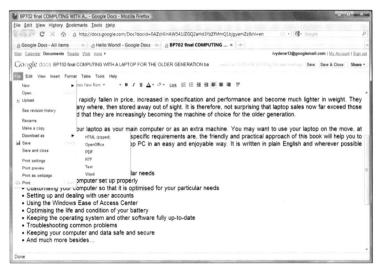

Fig.1.4 Documents can be downloaded in various formats

The usual facilities of a basic word processor are available when working on a document. If there is a menu bar near the top of the screen, as in Figure 1.3, this is the menu bar of the web browser, and not the one for the Google Docs word processor. This menu bar is situated in the conventional place, just above the main document area. It has the usual menus such as File, Edit, and Format. When you start using Google Docs it is easy to keep going to the wrong menu bar from force of habit, so it might be a good idea to switch off the browser's menu bar. A point to bear in mind when saving documents is that they are not saved on the hard disc drive of your computer, but are instead stored on a Google server. They can be loaded into Google Docs and edited using any computer that has Internet access. If you require hard copies of documents, they can be printed in the normal way using the Print option in the File menu.

Downloading documents

At some stage you might need to download a document to your computer, so that it can be used with a desktop publishing program perhaps. One way of doing this is to use the normal Copy and Paste facilities in the Google Docs Edit menu. With some browsers this will produce a warning message which explains that the Cut, Copy, and Paste facilitiesare not available from within Goggle Docs with the particular web browser in

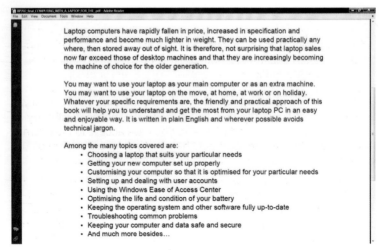

Laptop computers have rapidly fallen in price, increased in specification and performance and become much lighter in weight. They can be used practically any where, then stored away out of sight. It is therefore, not surprising that laptop sales now far exceed those of desktop machines and that they are increasingly becoming the machine of choice for the older generation.

You may want to use your laptop as your main computer or as an extra machine. You may want to use your laptop on the move, at home, at work or on holiday. Whatever your specific requirements are, the friendly and practical approach of this book will help you to understand and get the most from your laptop PC in an easy and enjoyable way. It is written in plain English and wherever possible avoids technical jargon.

Among the many topics covered are:
- Choosing a laptop that suits your particular needs
- Getting your new computer set up properly
- Customising your computer so that it is optimised for your particular needs
- Setting up and dealing with user accounts
- Using the Windows Ease of Access Center
- Optimising the life and condition of your battery
- Keeping the operating system and other software fully up-to-date
- Troubleshooting common problems
- Keeping your computer and data safe and secure
- And much more besides…

Fig.1.5 The test file has been successfully downloaded in PDF format

use. However, these facilities can still be used via the equivalent facilities in the browser's Edit menu, or using the normal Windows keyboard shortcuts. Of course, the same facilities can also be used if you need to import text into a Google Docs document.

The alternative is to download the document using the Download As option in the file menu. This has a submenu (Figure 1.4) which offers various file formats that provide compatibility with a wide range of application programs. There are the general Text and rich text formats (RTF), an HTML option, Word and OpenOffice word processor formats, and even the option of downloading the document in Adobe PDF format. When you use the Download As facility you will get the browser's normal pop-up window for handling downloads. This will usually offer the options of saving the file to disc or opening it in the default program for the selected file format. In Figure 1.5 I have opted to download the file in PDF format and open it in Adobe Reader.

Constant Email

Web-based Email and messaging systems are already familiar to a high percentage of computer users, and have become increasingly popular in recent years. Why do so many people use web-based Email systems such as Yahoo and Hotmail when it is normal to be supplied with several Email addresses when an account is opened with an Internet service provider? I think the most likely reason is that the Email addresses provided by your Internet service provider (ISP) are dependent on the account remaining open. If you switch to a different ISP, as most people tend to do from time-to-time, the Email addresses effectively cease to exist and can no longer be accessed. This is not a problem with an Internet based Email system such as Yahoo or Hotmail, where your Email addresses are not quite immortal, but could well outlive you. Even if you change your ISP annually, your web based Email account will carry on as normal, and can be used whenever you have access to the Internet. The contents of your Emails should be equally secure whether you use an account with your ISP or one with an established web Email service.

When choosing an Email service provider it is advisable to choose one that is likely to remain in business for many years to come, which in practice probably means choosing one of the large and well established services such as those provided by Yahoo!, Microsoft and Google. These larger companies often include other services as part of the deal, but they are optional and you can use only the Email service if that is all you require. These services are all free incidentally, and it seems likely that they will remain so into the foreseeable future.

Signing up to an Email service is usually very straight forward. The home page of the company will usually have a "Sign-up" link displayed fairly prominently. It will usually be necessary to provide a certain amount of personal information on the sign-up page, but there should be nothing too intrusive. You are usually free to choose the part of the Email address that appears to the left of the "@" sign, so there is plenty of scope to choose something eminently suitable. Unfortunately, with a well established Email company there will be many millions of existing Email addresses, and this can make it difficult to find something suitable. Rather than (say) "bobpenfold@" it might be necessary to settle for something more like "bobpenfold345@".

Email Search

There is a potential problem if you opt to keep every valid Email, and this is simply that you will eventually have a huge number of Emails stored in the system. This can make it difficult to find the one you need, especially if it was sent or received months or years ago. Web based Email systems have become more sophisticated in recent years, and there is usually a Search facility that can be used to hunt through all the stored Emails and search for a key word or several words. These systems operate in the standard search engine fashion. The example of Figure 1.6 shows the Google system in operation, and it has successfully located the two

Fig.1.6 The search system has located two Emails

Emails that contain the specified word. As in this case, there will usually be two versions of the Search facility, with one checking through your Emails and the other providing a normal web search, so make sure that you use the right one.

No POP3

Modern web based Email programs are quite sophisticated, and there are more facilities available than can be covered here. There are usually facilities for importing contacts from other Email systems and programs for example. There is one big omission though. Although it used to be quite common for web based Email systems to have a facility for connecting to an Email program such as Outlook or Outlook Express using a system known as POP3, this no longer seems to be the case. It is sometimes possible by upgrading to an account where a subscription is paid, but it does not seem to be a feature of the free Email services. Most free web based Email systems are strictly web based, with no option to use a conventional Email program running on your PC. You can use the copy facility to transfer the contents of an Email to another program, and the browser's usual facilities for saving and printing pages should

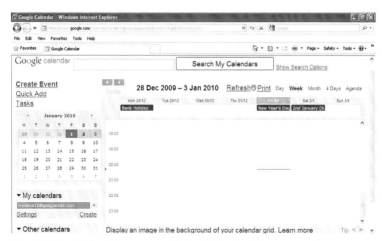

Fig.1.7 The Calendar program defaults to showing one week

be available, but there will probably be no other means of linking the Email system to the outside world.

Calendars

When in the Google Email system it is possible to access the Google Calendar facility via a link near the top left-hand corner of the screen. Alternatively, it can be access by going to:

www.google.com/calendar

If not already signed in to the Google system, it will be necessary to sign in before proceeding further. Some information has to be provided on the first occasion that you use the Calendar software, and this is mainly required in order to ensure that the right time zone is used. Once into the Calendar program (Figure 1.7) it will default to displaying one week, with the cells for each day having one hour increments. However, the tabs also provide options for showing one day, a month or four days, with the cell time changing to suit. For example, the one month option has one cell per day. The Google Calendar program is not just for producing calendars, and it is really intended as a means of keeping track of your appointments, or "events" as they are called in Google terminology. There is more than one way of adding an event, but the most simple is to first double-click on the appropriate cell. This produces a pop-up window (Figure 1.8) where details of the event are added. The

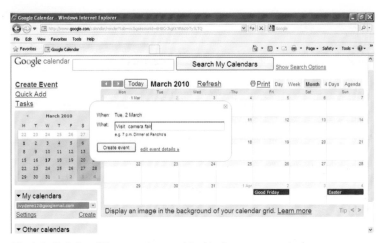

Fig.1.8 Details of the event are added in the pop-up window

newly added event will be blue in colour. The red coloured events are the standard ones such as public holidays that have been included by the program. An alternative method is to activate the Create Event link near the top left-hand corner of the window, and then add the appropriate information to the form that appears.

Agenda

The Agenda tab is very useful and it provides a simple list of events (Figure 1.9). It is worth investigating the Settings window, which is accessed via the link near the bottom left-hand corner of the normal window. This enables things such as the time and date format to be altered, the default view to be changed, and so on.

A similar facility is available from a Microsoft Email account such as one with Hotmail. Activating the Calendar link switches to this facility, and a small amount of information has to be entered when using the program for the first time. Tabs provide the option of viewing a day, a week, or one month, and the one month view is obtained by default. Double-clicking a cell brings up a small window where details of the event can be entered (Figure 1.10). With this calendar software the new events are shown in green. The blue events are public holidays that are supplied by the program. The tabs provide an agenda (Figure 1.11), and there is also one for producing a "to do" list.

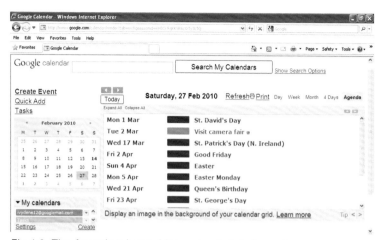

Fig.1.9 The Agenda tab provides a simple list of events

Spreadsheet

When in Google Docs there is a "Create new" menu near the top left-hand corner of the window (Figure 1.2), and the available options include one for spreadsheets. Selecting this option brings up a conventional spreadsheet (Figure 1.12). This is actually quite a sophisticated piece of software, and a detailed description of it goes well beyond the scope of this book. If you need to use a spreadsheet program it is certainly worth

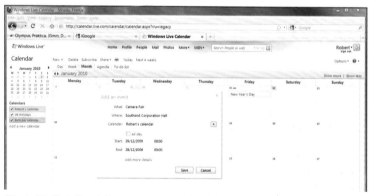

Fig.1.10 Details of the event are entered into the small pop-up window

Fig.1.11 An Agenda facility is available

trying this part of Google Docs. It can be used as a simple spreadsheet if that is all you need, but there are some advanced features as well. There are plenty of templates available for this software, and using something like "Google spreadsheet templates" in a search engine should provide numerous useful web pages. In many spreadsheet applications the ability to include charts without the need for a separate charting program is important. The current version of the Google spreadsheet program includes a very useful charting function (Figure 1.13).

Google Presentation

Another option under the "Create new" menu enables presentations to be produced. There is just one slide in place when the program is run,

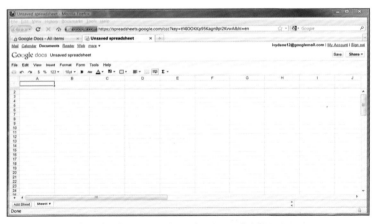

Fig.1.12 The Google Docs version of a spreadsheet

Fig.1.13 The Google Docs spreadsheet has a charting function

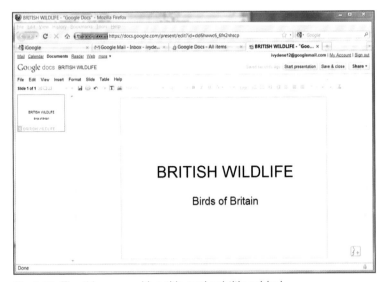

Fig.1.14 The title page with a title and subtitle added

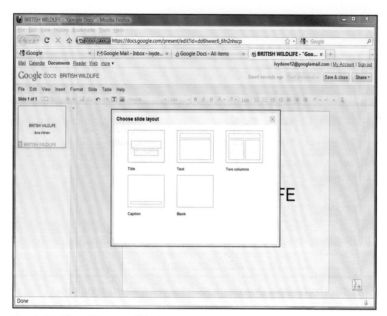

Fig.1.15 Five different slide layouts are available

and as one would probably expect, this is a title page. Here a title and subtitle are added (Figure 1.14), but if preferred it is possible to delete this page and add a different type. Assuming you wish to use the default starting page, there is the usual range of editing tools, so the font, text size, text colour, etc., can be changed. The next slide is added by either operating the "+" button near the top left-hand corner of the window, or by selecting "New slide" from the Slide menu. You are then offered a choice of five different slide layouts (Figure 1.15). For this example I chose the Caption layout, and then added an image and a caption to the new slide (Figure 1.16). Images are added using the appropriate button in the toolbar, or by using the Insert menu. The latter also enables other objects such as text, videos and tables to be added. The usual handles enable objects to be moved on the page and resized.

Bear in mind that when you use something like an image stored on your computer it is being uploaded to and stored on a Google server. Consequently, loading a high resolution image, or any other object that has a large file size, can be relatively slow. This is something that is to a large extent dependent on the upload speed of your Internet connection,

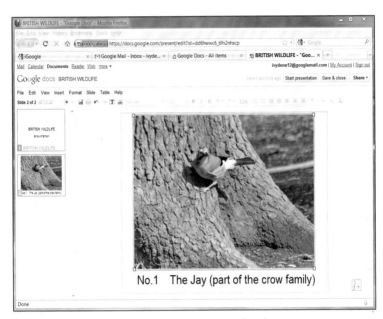

Fig.1.16 An example slide with a caption and an image

but the upload rate is often very much less than the download speed. Therefore, it is advisable to keep the file sizes of objects to the minimum that will do the job well. There is no point in uploading a ten megapixel image if it will only be used at one megapixel by a cloud application program. It is better to produce a smaller copy of about the right size and then upload that instead of the high resolution original. Always keep the higher resolution version of the image just in case you need a high quality version of it some time.

Another slide is then added, and the presentation is gradually built up. A thumbnail version of each slide appears in the left-hand column of the window, and the order of the slides can be changed by dragging their thumbnails to new positions. Right-clicking on one of the thumbnails brings up a menu that includes an option to delete it, move it up or down, or duplicate it. In general, adding content and editing it operates in standard Windows fashion, and it is quite easy to build up a presentation. The completed presentation can be downloaded in PDF, text, or PowerPoint format using the "Download as" option in the File

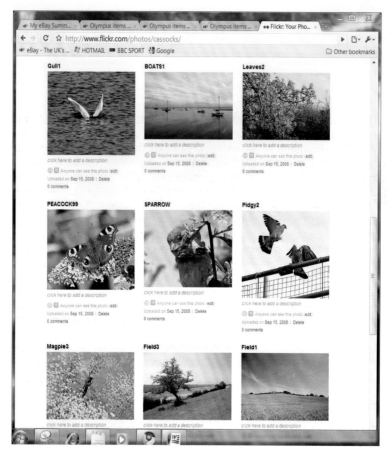

Fig.1.17 A photo album on Flickr.com

menu.

The rest

It is not possible to cover the full range of cloud computing applications here, since the range is now so vast. Google Docs includes a facility for producing forms, there are sites that provide facilities for producing web pages or even complete web sites, and there are online photo album sites such as Flickr.com (Figure 1.17), and so on. There is probably a cloud computing version of practically every popular type of application program.

Free software

Why Pay?

The amount of free software that is available to PC users seems to be one of the most closely guarded secrets in the world of computing. Few PC users, including those with years of experience with PCs, seem to appreciate the quality and depth of the software that can be downloaded free of charge. It would be an exaggeration to say that any type of software can be obtained in at least one good free version, but all the main software categories seem to be catered for, together with some software for niche applications. The reputation of free software is perhaps still tarnished by the low quality of most free software in the early days of PCs. Much of the software was incomplete, and was never completed, and it also had more than its fair share of bugs. It was also difficult to use, although I suppose that this was also true of most early software for PCs. The situation is much better these days, and while there is plenty of free software that is worth what you pay for it!, there are also some top quality programs available at no cost. It is certainly worth seeking out and trying some free software before buying commercial equivalents. You could save yourself a few hundred pounds initially, and potentially even more than this over a period of time because there will be no need to periodically pay for upgrades.

No support

It is only fair to point out that free software usually has a significant drawback in comparison to commercial equivalents. When you buy a commercial program it usually comes complete with some sort of free support. The quality of the support provided by the manufacturer varies significantly from one program to another, but it should be sufficient to enable you to get the software installed and running properly. It should also provide answers to simple queries about using the software. With free software there will usually be little or no support, but these days there is usually an online or downloadable instruction manual and (or) a built-in Help system that will answer many queries. Also, many programs are supported by online forums where experienced users give newcomers the benefit of their experience. Therefore, even though there may be no formal support for a free program, it is usually possible to obtain the answers to any problems that you experience.

Is it really free?

Using an Internet search engine it is not difficult to locate hundreds or even thousands of supposedly free programs. However, investigating the programs on offer usually reveals that a large proportion of them are not exactly free. For the purposes of this chapter a free program is one that is free to download, is fully working, and usable in the real world. Many of the available programs are some form of trial software or shareware. These programs will often run normally for a certain period of time that is typically about 30 days, but then some major restrictions come into operation, or the software simply ceases to work at all. Other programs will run indefinitely, but have some major restrictions right from the start. For example, there might be a limit on the maximum file size, the option to print files might be disabled, or it might not be possible to save files to disc. Some programs are so-called "lite" versions of commercial software. Some of these are perfectly usable, but many are so basic that they are of no practical use.

There are yet other types of free software, such as the type that is supported by pop-up advertising. Some programs are fully operational and will run indefinitely, but you will get a "nag screen" each time the program is run, extolling the virtues of the commercial version of the program. More of the screens might appear while the software is in use. The programs covered here do not fall into any of these categories, and are genuinely free, although with some you might get the occasional screen that pops up with some sort of special offer if you upgrade to the normal commercial version of the program.

Office suite

The OpenOffice suite from OpenOffice.org is probably the best known of the free office suites. This set of programs was formerly known as StarOffice. It is open source software, which means that it goes beyond simply being free. Unlike commercial software, where the source code for programs is a closely guarded secret and altering it is definitely not allowed, with open source software the program code is made available and you are free to modify it. This fact is probably of purely academic interest to most users as they will lack the expertise to alter the program, and it is the fact that it is genuinely free that is of primary importance to the majority of users. The OpenOffice suite provides several functions including word processing, spreadsheets, presentations, graphics and databases. These are not basic programs of limited practical use. They are sophisticated pieces of software that are usable in real-world applications, and the range of facilities provided is very impressive.

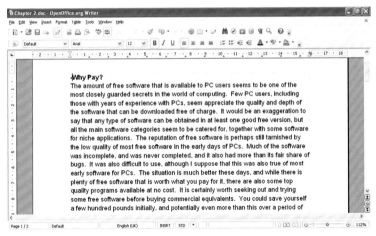

Fig.2.1 A Word DOC file opened in OpenOffice Writer

OpenOffice Writer

Writer is the word processor in the OpenOffice suite, and its "look and feel" is often likened to a version of Microsoft's Word from a few years ago. You should certainly find Writer easy to use if you are familiar with a version of Word prior to the ones having the "ribbon" user interface. One of the attractions of Writer for many users is that it can load and save files in several popular formats. There is no problem in loading Word files in either the old DOC format or the newer DOCX type, and they can be saved in several DOC versions. In Figure 2.1 I have loaded a Word DOC file straight into the program with no conversion process or any form of intermediate processing being required. It can also use the RTF, HTML, and Open Document 1.1 formats. It has the very useful ability of being able to export documents in the popular PDF format. Again, this is achieved from within the program with no add-ons or intermediate processing being required.

The program has the usual facilities for formatting text, plus some more advanced features such as macros, templates, collaborative features, and the option of using a spelling and grammar checker that analyses text as it is entered. OpenOffice Writer should be more than adequate for home use, and it should be adequate for many small businesses. It is free, so it is well worth trying this program before buying expensive commercial alternatives.

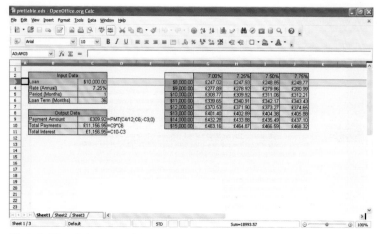

Fig.2.2 The Calc spreadsheet program

Probably most users of OpenOffice are primarily interested in the word processor, but the other normal office programs are there if you need them. These are the Calc spreadsheet (Figure 2.2), the Draw graphics program (Figure 2.3), the Impress presentation software (Figure 2.4), and the Base database program (Figure 2.5). The Draw graphics program

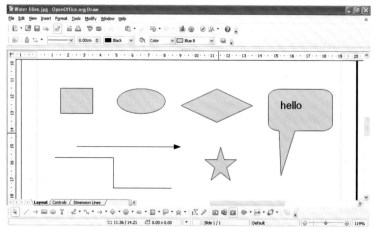

Fig.2.3 The OpenOffice Draw graphics program

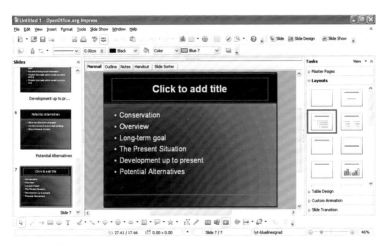

Fig.2.4 The Impress presentation program

seems to be mainly intended for producing business charts, and it is probably of limited value for photo editing and general illustration tasks. However, as explained next, there are other free programs available that can handle these applications.

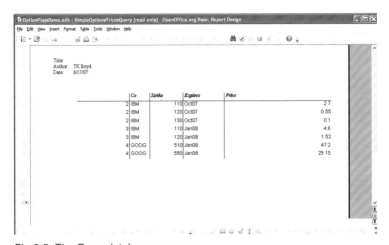

Fig.2.5 The Base database program

Fig.2.6 Picasa is a basic but useful photo editing program

Picasa photo editor

Digital cameras are often supplied complete with some photo-editing software, but it is not always included, and the quality of the supplied software varies enormously. Some of it is excellent, while in other cases the range of available features is strictly limited. A few of the bundled photo-editing programs are actually quite powerful, but are of limited practical value as they are difficult and cumbersome to use. Google's Picasa software (Figure 2.6) is a good choice if the software included with your camera is not up to the task or you find it impossible to use effectively. The size of the download is a little less than twelve megabytes, so it should pose no problems even if you have a dial-up Internet connection.

It is straightforward in use and has a useful range of features including red-eye reduction, cropping, sharpening, filter effects, exposure adjustments, a basic retouching facility, and straightening (rotation). There is also an "I'm Feeling Lucky" option that will try to optimise photographs automatically, with no manual input. As with any system of this type, results tend to be a bit mixed. However, it only takes one click of the mouse to undo the processing if the instant fix provided is not to your liking. The program also has a basic but useful library feature (Figure 2.7) that can locate all the photographs stored on your PC and make it reasonably easy to find the ones you require.

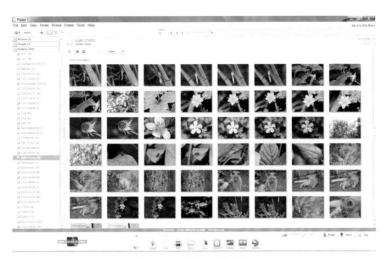

Fig.2.7 Picasa has a useful photo library facility

Illustration with Inkscape

A vector graphics program is one that does not operate primarily with bit maps and pixels, but instead deals in terms of objects such as lines, circles, rectangles, and other shapes. It can handle simple and complex fills for those shapes. The main point of using this type of graphics program is that it can produce very high quality output with a suitable output device. With a bit map the quality that can be provided is limited by the resolution of the bit map. The output quality of a vector graphics program is limited by the capabilities of the output device used, and not by the program or the drawings produced using that program. Adobe illustrator and CorelDraw are the two best known commercial programs of this type. The range of free alternatives to these programs is limited, and there is probably no free program that genuinely rivals them, but Inkscape (Figure 2.8) has sufficient facilities to satisfy many users. It has a good range of basic objects, fill types, text capabilities, and so on, and it is capable of producing high quality output. This is another open source program incidentally.

GIMP

GIMP (GNU image manipulation program) is perhaps the best known of the free graphics programs, which is perhaps a little surprising as it is primarily a program for the Linux operating system. At least one Windows version is available though (Figure 2.9). It is a paint program that also

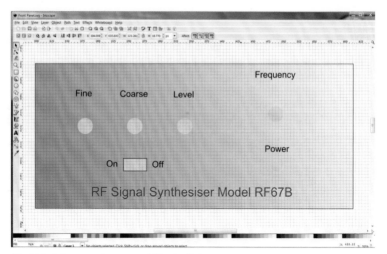

Fig.2.8 Inkscape is a good illustration program

has photo editing features, rather like Adobe's Photoshop software. While it lacks the huge range of features available from Photoshop, it is still a very complex program that has a massive range of features. Due to its popularity it is well documented though, and it has a built-in help system and user manual. There is also a huge amount of information about using this program to be found on the Internet.

Visual BASIC Express

There are numerous free programming languages available, although many of them seem to be quite old and probably of relatively little practical use in modern computing. This is not true of Visual BASIC Express, which at the time of writing this piece has reached the 2010 edition (Figure 2.10). It is effectively the full commercial but most basic version of the Visual BASIC programming language. The version intended for beginners used to cost nearly one hundred pounds and there were major limitations on the way in which any programs written with this software could be distributed. Any form of commercial distribution was forbidden, and required the user to buy the more advanced but also much more expensive professional version. The Express version of Visual BASIC does not have this restriction, and normal commercial distribution of the software produced using this program is permitted. A full-time professional programmer will certainly need one of the full commercial

Fig.2.9 GIMP has paint and photo editing features

versions, but the Express edition is probably all that will be needed for occasional amateur or professional use.

Visual BASIC has become more sophisticated over the years, but one drawback of the increasing sophistication is that it is not as easy to use as the original versions. Due to its popularity there is plenty of information and tutorials available on the Internet, in addition to the substantial amount of support information provided by Microsoft themselves. Being realistic about matters though, it will probably be necessary to obtain a good beginners book on this programming language in order to get the most from it. The recent versions of Visual BASIC have a major limitation compared to earlier versions, which is that they lack the drawing components that used to make it so easy to add and control lines and simple shapes. Fortunately, there is a free add-on called Power Packs 3 that, amongst other things, adds this facility to Visual BASIC 2010. It is worth noting that the other programming languages in Microsoft's Visual Studio suite are available as free Express editions, or you can simply download and install the Express edition of the complete Visual Studio suite. The other languages are Visual C++, Visual C#, and Visual Web developer. These are mostly quite large downloads, so they might not be a practical proposition using a dial-up connection. Note that the Microsoft Express edition programs will only run for 30 days unless they are registered, but the registration process is free.

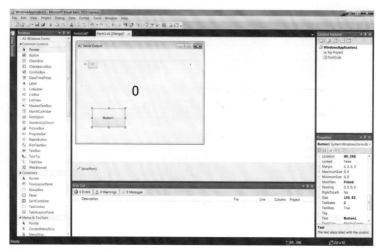

Fig.2.10 Visual BASIC 2010 Express is a complex piece of software

Web browsers

Windows comes complete with a sophisticated web browser in the form of Internet Explorer. However, with Windows 7 you are offered the choice of downloading and using an alternative browser, and there is now a surprisingly large range of web browsers programs to choose from. Of course, there is no point in changing to a different browser just for the sake of it. It makes sense to carry on using Internet Explorer if you are happy with its facilities, and the later versions have a useful range of features including tabs. Some web sites, and particularly the financial type, seem to need Internet Explorer to function properly, so you need to have this browser available even if you use a different one for surfing the Internet.

Probably the most common reason for changing to a different web browser is that Internet Explorer can be slow to load, and with some computers it does not run particularly quickly. Unfortunately, the same seems to be true of some browsers that were once very undemanding, but have grown with each new release. Google's Chrome browser program (Figure 2.11) is relatively new, and while it might eventually suffer from so-call "software bloat", at the moment it offers a useful range of features while running quite fast on computers that have a fairly basic specification.

Fig.2.11 Google's Chrome browser is gaining in popularity

CCleaner

There are numerous utility programs for use with Windows, offering facilities such as Windows Registry scanning and cleaning, disc defragmentation, and the removal of unnecessary files from the hard disc drive. You have to be especially careful with this type of software since it can seriously damage the operating system if it is not written properly. Also, bogus utility software has long been a popular way

Fig.2.12 The CCleaner Registry scanner

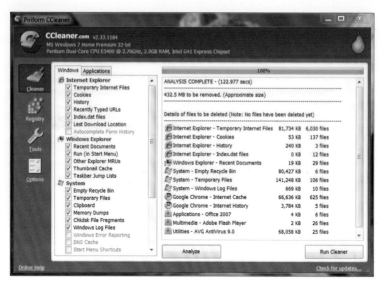

Fig.2.13 The disc clean-up section of CCleaner

of attacking computers and infecting them with viruses, Trojans, spyware, and other malicious software. Another point to bear in mind is software of this type can do more harm than good unless it is written specifically for the particular version of Windows in use. Before downloading and installing any software of this type you need to ensure that it is of reasonable quality, and download sites that include software reviews can be very helpful here. It is also best to download it from a reliable source, and check carefully that it is recommended for use with the version of Windows installed on your PC.

CCleaner is a popular utility program that has a good track record. Amongst other things it can be used to check for errors in the Windows Registry (Figure 2.12), and in most cases it can fix any errors that are found. It can also check the hard disc drives for unnecessary files (Figure 2.13), and erase the selected files to free hard disc space. In this example it found about 435 megabytes of temporary files, etc., that were not needed.

Ubuntu Linux

It is not only application programs that are available as free downloads. There are even free operating systems as well, and the various versions of Linux are by far the most popular. Linux started life as an alternative to

Fig.2.14 Ubuntu Linux is a popular distribution at present

the Unix operating system, and it was a text based system, rather like the old MS-DOS operating system but more advanced. These days it is normally operated in conjunction with additional software that provides a WIMP (windows, icons, mouse, and pointer) environment, like Windows. Many modern versions of Linux are reasonably easy to use, and most distributions come complete with large amounts of free software. Bear in mind though, that this is a complex operating system and it can be difficult to sort things out if something goes awry.

Ubuntu Linux is probably the most popular version of Linux at present, and it is a good choice for those who are new to the Linux operating system. It is possible to download the image of a bootable CD that can be used to try Ubuntu Linux without installing it on a computer (Figure 2.14). It can also be installed normally as the sole operating system on a computer, or it can be installed alongside Windows in a dual boot system. One slight problem when downloading a Linux operating system and the application programs to go with it, is the size of the download which is usually measured in gigabytes rather than megabytes. Even if you have a fast broadband Internet connection, it might be more practical to buy the installation discs.

Finding free software

It is only possible to cover a few of the more popular free programs here, and a large number of free but good programs are available. One way of finding free software for a given application is to go to a specialist software download site such as Brothersoft.com or Download.com. Sites of this type usually have the programs sorted into categories and subcategories so that it is relatively quick and easy to find programs of the appropriate type. There should also be at least a basic search facility. However, bear in mind that these sites usually cover any software that can be downloaded without charge. Most of the software on offer will be shareware, commercial trials, and the like, rather than fully usable software that is free. You therefore need to carefully check the exact type of software you are dealing with before going ahead and installing it.

The web sites of magazines sometimes have sections where various free programs are available as downloads. It is not just computer magazines that provide a service of this type, and with (say) a magazine for photographers there might be a selection of imaging related software available from the web site. Although the range of software on offer will usually be quite small, it should be fully tried and tested and will usually be of good quality. Using something like "best free software" as the search string in a search engine should provide links to a number of sites that list a range of top quality free programs. There will usually be short reviews that give you some idea of the suitability of programs before you download them. Some sites also carry reviews from people who have tried the programs. These can help you to avoid wasting time downloading programs that will fall short of your requirements.

Take due care

Any good search engine should be able to locate some suitable free software if you use a well chosen search string, with the obvious proviso that the required software actually exists as a free download. This is a more risky way of doing things since it will sometimes involve moving away from tried, tested, and trustworthy sites to smaller sites that are something of an "unknown quantity". Take due care, and if in doubt you should not be tempted to download and install the software on offer.

URLs

I have deliberately avoided providing URLs for the programs mentioned in this chapter, because it seems to be the norm for new addresses to pop up and old ones disappear. The best way to find the current download address is to use the name of the program and "download" as the search terms in any good Internet search engine.

Downloading

Downloading large files is an application where the speed of a broadband Internet connection is certainly a great asset. Downloading a few hundred megabytes of data using a real-world dial-up connection would take many hours, and might never be completed successfully. Even using a relatively slow broadband connection it would probably take less than an hour to download the same amount of data, and with the fastest of broadband connections it would require a matter of minutes rather than hours. Of course, in real-world computing matters are never as straightforward as that, and downloading large files using a fast Internet connection will not always be "plain sailing". The download speed is governed by the slowest part of the system. This will almost invariably be your Internet connection when using a dial-up type.

It is by no means a foregone conclusion that the Internet connection will be the limiting factor when using some form of broadband connection. As the speed of broadband connections has steadily increased over the years, the rest of the Internet has not always kept up with developments. The practical result of this is that file servers and the Internet infrastructure may not always be able to equal the download speed of your Internet connection. The faster your Internet service, the less likely it is that the other parts of the system will be able to keep up with it. With a fast broadband connection you are at least in a position to make the most of the available speed from the rest of the Internet, whatever that happens to be.

With a dial-up connection you are limited to a slow download rate, and there is no way around that limitation. You can set things up in such a way as to make the most of the limited speed that is available, but do not be hoodwinked into thinking that a few tricks and tips or some special software will give broadband speed from a dial-up connection. A dial-up connection is intrinsically slow, and there is no way around that limitation.

While there can be problems with the equipment between your PC and the server, in practice it seems to be problems with the servers that give the most trouble when trying to download at high speed. The server is the computer system that stores the Internet pages you visit, or files that you download. There is a limit to the workload that the server can handle efficiently, and there is also a limit on the speed at which it can upload data to the Internet. Some servers are highly sophisticated and can easily accommodate a large number of users simultaneously, while others are just ordinary PCs that are quite old. Similarly, some servers connect to the Internet via what is essentially just an ordinary broadband connection of some type, while others have hi-tech connections with massive bandwidths.

Unfortunately, the fact that you are dealing with an up-market server that has a super-fast link to the Internet does not mean that it will always be able to supply data to your PC at a high rate. Neither does it follow that a primitive server with a more modest link to the Internet will always be slow at providing data. An important factor is the number of users accessing the server. You may well get quick service if you are the only person accessing a relatively slow server, but only a slow download rate if you are one of several thousand people using the latest hi-tech server. At times when a server is busy you may therefore find that the maximum download rate is far less than the highest rate that your Internet connection can accommodate. In fact some servers limit the number of users to a figure that enables each user to receive a fairly high download rate, so some download services simply become unavailable at times of high demand.

This is a bit inconvenient from the user's point of view, but in most cases it is possible to go ahead with the download if you try again later. There can be a more serious problem with sites that utilise low-cost or free web hosting services. The hosts of some web sites place limits on the total amount of data that can be downloaded per month. Sites that make use of this form of economy hosting can therefore be unavailable for several days if they suddenly become very popular and the month's download allocation is reached before the end of the month. With this type of thing you just have to keep checking the web site so that you can access the file you require as soon as it goes back online.

The time is right

One way of avoiding problems with overloaded servers is to download files at times when demand is likely to be low. Judging when demand will be low can be a bit problematic though. There should be no difficulty if the site is one that is only likely to be of interest to people living in your own country. Demand is likely to be very low from late in the evening through to early the next morning. Depending on whether it is a business or leisure oriented site, the peak demand is likely to be in the afternoon or evenings. There may be no real slack period with a site that has users all over the world, since there will always be plenty of users in one part of the world or another. Practical experience suggests that in the UK, many sites seem to be at their best in the early morning before 9-00 AM. However, it might be necessary to try awkward sites at various times of the day in order to find a time when the required files can be downloaded efficiently.

Download managers

There are programs that are designed to manage and in some cases speed up downloads. Programs of this type are generally called download managers. One advantage of these programs is that they will usually be able to resume a broken download, carrying on from the point at which the download stopped. The built-in download facility of a browser might lack this facility, making it necessary to start again from the beginning if the connection to the server is lost. This is a less severe problem than it used to be, since modern browsers have a built-in download manager that is usually fairly basic but is still capable of resuming a broken download.

Broken downloads are not a major problem with broadband connections, since the reliability is generally much higher than that obtained when using a typical dial-up connection. Also, the time taken to download a given amount of data is much less, giving less time for things to go wrong. However, things can still go awry from time-to-time, and some servers operate with something well short of one hundred percent reliability. The ability to resume broken downloads is certainly a very worthwhile facility. Note though, that it is a facility that can only work if it is supported by the equipment at both ends of the link. Therefore, the fact that you are using a download manager does not mean that it will always be possible to resume broken downloads. Fortunately, these days the vast majority of servers support this feature.

Optimum speed

The more sophisticated download managers try to ensure that files are always downloaded at the highest possible rate, and programs of this type are sometimes called "download accelerators". There are two main approaches to optimising download speeds. One of these is to test the various sources of the file so that the fastest server or servers can be used. Files are often available from a main site and various secondary sites, or "mirror" sites as they are termed. The chances of finding mirror sites depend on the popularity of the file you are trying to download. With a very popular download there could be dozens of alternative sites available, but with less popular files there will usually be no mirror servers available, making this method inapplicable.

Pinging

The speed of servers is usually gauged using a method known as "pinging". Pinging is sending a small packet of data to a server and back again. The shorter the time this takes the faster the download is likely to be. It tends to be assumed that the rate at which data can be downloaded is purely dependent on the speed of the connection to the Internet service provider and the speed at which the server can send data. However, data is not downloaded from the server in the form of one continuous stream of data. It is sent in smaller chunks called "packets", and a dialogue is needed between your PC and the server in order to ensure that everything works smoothly. Time is lost each time your PC and the server try to establish contact. Pinging is used to measure how quickly (or otherwise) your PC and the server can establish contact, rather than just measuring the rate at which data can be transferred between the two. With a short ping time there is relatively little time wasted trying to establish contact so that messages or packets of data can be exchanged efficiently.

Multiple threads

Checking for the fastest site seems to be used much less than in the past, and most download accelerators rely mainly on the use of multiple threads. This is probably the most effective method of accelerating a download. Suppose that you have an Internet connection that can handle a maximum download rate of eight megabits per second, but a server will only supply one megabit per second. With the multiple thread approach to things the download manager divides the file into (say) four equal parts which it then simultaneously downloads from the server. Having downloaded all four sections it then joins them to produce the complete file. The point of using four simultaneous downloads is that, with luck, each part of the file will download at one megabit per second. This gives an effective download rate of four megabits per second. In practice it is unlikely that the download rate would be accelerated to quite this degree, since there are minor inefficiencies in the system, and using four threads increases the loading on the server. Even so, the

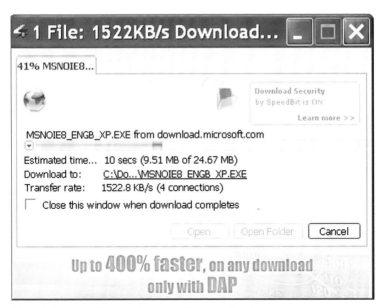

Fig.3.1 Accelerator Plus is a popular download manager

download rate would typically be increased by a factor of nearly four, which would provide a large reduction in download times.

Of course, the multiple-thread method of downloading is of little help in cases where the server is providing data at a high rate. In fact it might reduce efficiency and produce a slight reduction in the download rate when used with a fast server. Not all servers will permit more than one connection per IP address, so it will not always be an option. Some servers permit multiple connections, but with a limit of two or three per IP address. Many FTP servers only permit one or two connections per user, but the more usual HTTP types are generally more accommodating. Where the server is a bit slow, even one extra connection still permits a very worthwhile increase in download speed. The multiple thread method is unlikely to be of any use with a dial-up connection because the speed of the Internet connection is likely to be low in comparison to the speed of the server. For it to be of any assistance the Internet connection must be significantly faster than the speed of the server. The popular Download Accelerator Plus program is shown in action in Figure 3.1, and using four connections it is achieving a very impressive download rate.

Windows optimising

Some download manager programs have facilities to optimise various Windows settings so that the fastest possible download rate is achieved. There are also special optimiser programs and numerous Internet sites that give advice on this subject. In general, there is probably no point in most Internet users bothering with this type of thing. Provided a suitably high download rate is achieved when using a fast server there is not really a lot to be gained by experimenting with some of the Windows settings. Altering settings in the Windows Registry has to be regarded as a little risky, and it is possible to do serious damage to the operating system if you make a major error.

I suppose the situation is rather different if you consistently obtain download rates that are well short of the maximum theoretical rate for your Internet connection. When this occurs it is probably best to contact your Internet service provider first in order to check that you are connected at the correct speed and that there is no problem with their hardware. They should be able to suggest some checks that can be made at your end of the system to determine what is wrong. It is perhaps worth resorting to optimising techniques if the download rates still seem rather low.

Quoted speeds

Bear in mind that most broadband connections rely on equipment that is shared with a number of other users. Download rates can be significantly reduced at times when several users are downloading files or engaging in other activities that require a large amount of bandwidth. The distance from your premises to the telephone exchange is also an important factor with broadband that uses ordinary telephone cables. The greater this distance, the lower the likely speed of your Internet connection. Remember that the connection speeds quoted by Internet service providers are the maximum obtainable speeds, and that for most users the actual connection speed will be significantly less.

Peer-to-peer

Vast amounts of data are swapped over the Internet using peer-to-peer (P2P) networks. The MP3 format and using a computer to play music first became big news when the original Napster site was launched. This enabled users to look at the music available on the hard disc drives of other users and download anything that took their fancy. The problem with this system, or any similar system, is that there is no reliable way of preventing users from illegally swapping material that is protected by copyright. After a number of legal wrangles the original Napster was taken over and eventually turned into a site providing legal music downloads. Note that the original site at www.napster.com is only for US residents. However, there is a UK version at www.napster.co.uk.

Napster was an early example of a peer-to-peer network, which is a term used to describe any system that enables users to share each others data via the Internet. Although the original Napster no longer exists, there are plenty of peer-to-peer file sharing programs available, and some of them are available as free downloads. The companies behind some of these programs are embroiled in ongoing legal disputes with the recording companies and organisations that represent them. Some peer-to-peer programs have been discontinued as a result of these legal wrangles. A peer-to-peer program can be used for legitimate file swapping, but it can also be used for illegally swapping material that is still in copyright. This has made peer-to-peer systems something of a "grey area", since they are legal or illegal depending on how they are used.

Peer-to-peer problems

If you use a peer-to-peer file sharing system it is important to bear in mind that there are potential problems. A substantial amount of the material available on the popular systems seems to be within copyright and downloading it is illegal. Perhaps of greater importance, making this type of thing available for others to download from your computer is also illegal and has resulted in prosecutions in the US and the UK. When using peer-to-peer systems it is important to make sure that you do not download or make available anything that cannot be swapped legitimately.

Downloading files via a peer-to-peer network can be problematic. It is very easy to end up with an incomplete file that can never be fully downloaded, or a complete but badly corrupted and useless file. There are plenty of jokers operating on these systems, and one of their tricks is to put files on the system that are not what they are purported to be. Sometimes this is relatively innocent, with the downloaded file actually being a piece of music, a picture, or whatever kind of file you were trying to download, but the wrong one. In other cases the downloaded file is pornography, a file that is infected with a virus, a backdoor Trojan, or something of this general type. You need to be on your guard if you use one of these systems, and they are probably not something that newcomers to computing should get involved in. Many experienced computer users refuse to have anything to do with peer-to-peer systems.

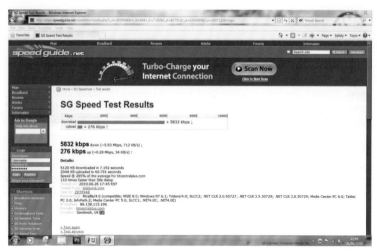

Fig.3.2 The www.speedguide.net site running its tests

Speed test

Should you feel that your Internet connection is falling "short of the mark", there are plenty of websites that will help you to test its speed. However, with anything of this type you have to remember that it is not, strictly

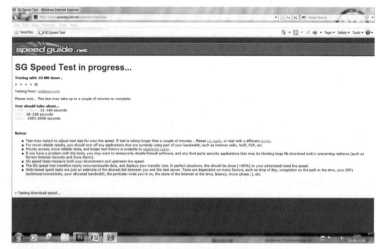

Fig.3.3 The speeds obtained were a little below par

Fig.3.4 Various sites around the world can be used for the speed test

speaking, the speed of your Internet connection that is being tested. What is actually being tested is the speed of your Internet connection, the server that hosts the test website, and the Internet infrastructure that connects the two. Consequently, you might get significantly different results if you try a range of speed testing sites. In fact it is highly likely that significant differences will be found.

For an initial test I tried the test site at www.speedguide.net, which ran through its tests (Figure 3.2) and then produced the results of Figure 3.3. The nominal download and upload speeds of the Internet connection used for this test were respectively eight megabits per second and 384 kilobits per second. The results produced by the test were a download speed of just over 5.8 megabits and an upload rate of 276 kilobits per second, which are both a bit disappointing. This test site enables a site close to your location to be selected (Figure 3.4), and the one I chose was probably no more than about 70 kilometres away. The point of doing this is that, in general, faster results are obtained using a server that is reasonably close. This should result in the data taking a reasonably direct route rather than doing a tour of the world's Internet hubs! However, there is no absolute guarantee that using a server that is close to your location will ensure a relatively direct link between the two ends of the system. It is still possible that the connection will be made via Internet hubs thousands of miles away, but this is highly unlikely.

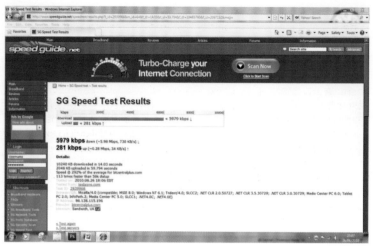

Fig.3.5 A second test produced slightly improved results

A probable cause of the slight shortfall in speed in this instance is that the link from the computer to the router was via a wi-fi link that was something less than perfect. It is better to carry out this type of test with the computer connected to the router via a cable, as this should not introduce any reduction in performance. Repeating the test with the computer hard-wired to the router gave slightly better results (Figure 3.5), but both speeds were significantly less than the theoretical maximums. Even so, the speeds obtained were perfectly acceptable, and adequate to provide good results in most applications. Repeating the tests at a different time of day produced upload and download speeds that were much closer to the theoretical maximum rates. If you try a few speed tests at different times of day and using a variety of test sites you should get a good idea of the sort of download rate you can expect from real-world sites.

File swapping

The speed of a broadband connection makes it possible to use the Internet as a means of sending large data files to other people. One slight snag is that the maximum upload speed of most broadband connections is far lower than the highest achievable download rate. It is often just 256 kilobits per second, and is unlikely to be more than 512 kilobits per second. The practical consequence of this is that it will usually take far longer for the sender to upload data than it does for the recipient to download it. However, unless hundreds of megabytes or more of data is involved, upload times should still be reasonable.

Attachments

There are numerous ways of exchanging data over the Internet, and the best option depends on the amount of data involved, how often data will have to be transferred, and the number of recipients. Email is becoming a very popular means of swapping files, but it can be difficult to exchange very large amounts of data using this method. The Emails themselves are of little use for swapping anything other than simple text files. However, practically any Email service should be able to handle attachments. These are simply files that are sent with an Email, and they can be opened or downloaded by the recipient. This way of working has obvious attractions, but the main advantage is the ease with which it can be implemented. Most people already have at least one Email address, making it possible to exchange files over the Internet with a minimum of fuss. There is no need to find any web space or to use any special software. You just use your existing Email account and software. Even if you would prefer not to use your main Email account for file swapping, there is no major problem. There are plenty of free Email services, and signing up to one of these takes very little time.

As pointed out previously, with many Email services it can be difficult to swap large amounts of data. Even with the more generous allowances of modern Email services, anything more than about 10 or 20 megabytes per Email is unlikely to be allowed. This is still more than adequate for many purposes though. The restrictions seem to be different for each service provider, so you have to check on the limits imposed by your particular provider prior to sending large amounts of data. Bear in mind that there might also be restrictions on what can be received by the system used by the recipient. If your Emails fail to meet any restrictions imposed by the receiving system, it is certain that some of the attachments will be filtered. It is also possible that all the attachments will be filtered.

Filtering problems

Internet security is now a major issue for users and providers of Internet services. One practical outcome of increased Email security is that some service providers do not permit certain types of file to be included as attachments. At the other end of the system, some providers will not accept attachments containing certain file types. Trying to send a file of a proscribed type will usually result in an error message. Sometimes a certain file type might be acceptable to your Email provider, but not to the recipient's provider. This will usually result in the attachment being filtered, and the recipient's service provider will then send you an Email explaining why the attachment has been filtered.

The file types that are most likely to be filtered are executable program files, such as those having EXE and COM extensions. Extensions to program files such as DLL types might also be prohibited. It is quite likely that you will never need to send any of the proscribed file types, but compressed files can sometimes cause problems. Most types of compressed files should be permissible, including those having the common filename extensions such as ZIP and RAR. It is the self-extracting files that are likely to cause problems. This type of file is a program file that usually has an EXE extension.

The file is actually a simple decompression utility plus the compressed data. Running the program results in the data being decompressed, and then it is stored in the folder specified by the user. This type of compressed file has the advantage of not requiring the recipient to have a decompression program of the appropriate type. There is a slight drawback in that including the decompression program with the data results in a larger file. When sending compressed files via Email it is better to use an ordinary type that does not include the decompression program. This should avoid problems with the file being filtered, and ensures that the amount of data sent is kept to a minimum.

Alternative methods

There are plenty of alternatives to using Email as a means of exchanging files, although these are probably only worthwhile where very large files are involved. Most ISPs provide their broadband customers with a certain amount of free web space as part of the package. The amount of space varies considerably from one company to another, and it is not always included as standard. Where some free web space is provided, there is usually a size limit of between five and one hundred megabytes.

A fairly small web space allocation is unlikely to be of much practical value when swapping files with others, since it requires more expertise than using the Email method, but does not provide any increase in the maximum file size than can be accommodated. The situation is different with a limit of around fifty or one hundred megabytes, which is far higher than can easily be handled using Email attachments. However, you are effectively making your own miniature website when using this method, which makes life easy for those downloading the files, but requires more expertise on the part of the person producing the website. A simple site of this type is not difficult to set up, and some ISPs even provide helpful utilities that aid the building of your own website. However, initially it will still require a bit more time and effort than using Email attachments.

An advantage of this system is that, where necessary, files can be distributed to a number of people with a minimum of effort. You only have to upload the files to the website once, and they can then be downloaded by each person that requires them. It is not necessarily true to say that there is no limit on the number of people that can download the files once they have been uploaded to your site, because ISPs often impose download or bandwidth caps, but this should only be a problem if you need to supply large files to dozens of people. There is a drawback in using your own website, which is that the files are not secure, and can be downloaded by anyone who knows where they are, or just happens to stumble across them. The Email method is not totally secure, but the website approach is not secure at all. Either it should not be used with files that are in any way of a sensitive nature, or the files should be encrypted.

Hosting service

It is possible to use file hosting services if your ISP does not provide plenty of free web space, or you do not feel that making your own website is a practical proposition. The cost of most file hosting services is quite low, and in some cases there is a free service that will suffice for most purposes. Probably the most popular of these services is RapidShare (www.rapidshare.com), which allows files of up to one hundred megabytes to be uploaded. Larger files can be accommodated by splitting and recombining files using a program such as Winrar.

Even with the free service, there is no limit on the number of files that can be uploaded. However, there are download limits for users who do not have a paid-for account. This works on the basis of having an enforced wait between the downloading of one file and the next. It is still possible to download a few hundred megabytes during the course of a day, which is perfectly adequate for most users.

Rapid uploading

Uploading to a free file hosting site is usually very straightforward, with no special software being required. An ordinary browser program such as Internet Explorer together with the built-in features of the host site is all that should be needed. In the case of RapidShare it is a matter of first going to the homepage (Figure 3.6). A short tutorial video is available in

Fig.3.6 The RapidShare.com homepage

the lower section of the window, but using this service is very easy and the video will probably not be needed. Start the uploading process by entering the path and filename of the file you wish to upload, or using the file browser to select the required file. Left-clicking the Upload button starts the transfer of the file to the server, and the data in the middle part of the window shows how things are progressing (Figure 3.7). Eventually the upload process will be completed, and the window will change to indicate that the server has received the file (Figure 3.8).

Rapid downloading

The middle section of the page shows the download address for your file, but there are actually two web addresses. One of these is used to download your file, while the other is used to delete it. With free accounts your files are automatically deleted after 60 days with no download activity, so it is not absolutely necessary to remove files once you have finished with them. However, doing so might be desirable from the security point of view, and it is good practice to delete files from websites once they

Fig.3.7 The upload process is under way

are not needed any more. This avoids unnecessarily occupying space on the server, and is the "good manners" thing to do when using free web space. Note that with the current Rapidshare rules, it is only possible to download a file ten times unless you register an account with RapidShare.

Fig.3.8 The file has been uploaded successfully

Fig.3.9 Non-account users should operate the Free user button

Fig.3.10 There is a delay before the download can commence

Fig.3.11 Operate the Download button to start the download

Make a note of the download address and the file to which it applies. It is obviously not possible to download a file without its download address, and this address must be supplied to everyone who will need to download the file. Note that the address provided is not a direct link to the file, but is one that takes users to the file via the RapidShare system. Using a RapidShare link produces a window like the one shown in Figure 3.9, and non-account holders can access the file by operating the Free button near the bottom of the window towards the right.

This moves things on to a page where a delay is enforced (Figure 3.10). There is no delay for users that have a paid-for RapidShare account, and it is presumably included for users of the free service to encourage them to upgrade. Free web services often have a simple security system of the type where you have to read and then enter a code, and this is done to prevent inappropriate use of the service using robot computer systems. However, this is not currently a feature of the RapidShare system. The window changes to look like Figure 3.11 once the countdown has finished, It is then just a matter of operating the Download button and going through the usual download procedure. In this case the file was a jpg image type, and it was opened in a new browser window (Figure 3.12).

Fig.3.12 The image file has been downloaded

Compression and splitting

The maximum file sizes permitted by file hosting services tend to be much larger than those allowed by Email services. It is usually possible to have files as large as one hundred megabytes, and in some cases the limit is two hundred megabytes. It is permissible to upload numerous files. I suppose that in exceptional cases the maximum file size allowed could be inadequate, but the ability to upload several files provides a solution to the problem. With something like an archive of video clips or images it is just a matter of collecting the files into smaller groups so that no group exceeds the maximum file size. Matters are trickier if the file to be uploaded is genuinely one file rather than an archive of several files. One potential way around the problem is to use a compression program such as WinRAR or WinZip to compress the file. Compression works quite well with some types of file, reducing the file size by about 50 to 70 percent. With other types of file, and particularly with those that already have some form of built-in compression, there can be little or no reduction in size. An alternative approach is to use a file splitter program to slice a large file into several smaller ones. The recipient then uses the same program to combine the pieces and reconstitute the original file. The WinRAR compression program has the ability to slice and recombine files, and there are programs that are designed specifically for this purpose.

eBay buying

Auction types

Buying goods on eBay is much easier than selling them, and you can get started almost straight away. You have to register an account with eBay, but you can then start bidding, or buying goods in a so-called "fixed price" auction. This is a contradiction of terms if ever there was one, and a fixed price auction is an auction where there is no bidding. Instead the listing has a Buy-it-Now button, and you can use this to buy the goods immediately. In other words, the goods are sold via what is really just an ordinary advertisement. Sometimes the Buy-it-Now option is included as part of a normal auction listing, giving the options of bidding or buying straight away. With this type of auction the Buy-it-Now option disappears when the first bid is placed, or when the reserve price is reached if the seller has set a reserve on the item. In most cases this means that the Buy-it-Now option disappears if you place a bid, but this is not necessarily the case if there is a reserve price. You might lose the item if you are outbid in the normal way, or someone could use the Buy-it-Now option, thus ending the auction. Note that sellers can state the reserve price on their listings, but few actually do so. Few will reveal the price if you ask them to do so using the eBay messaging facility. It can be useful to remember that the minimum reserve price on an eBay.co.uk auction is fifty pounds.

Best offer

There is a variation on the standard version of a fixed price auction, and this is the inclusion of a facility that enables an offer to be sent to the seller. Depending on how the seller has set up the listing, an offer will be automatically accepted or declined, or sent to the seller for their consideration. The listing remains active if your offer is sent to the seller, and it is not put "on hold" until the seller reaches a decision. If someone uses the Buy-it-Now option during this time your offer is automatically declined and the listing closes. Others can make offers while yours is being considered, and once again, your offer is automatically declined and the listing closes if the seller accepts a better offer. Offers expire after 48 hours should the seller fail to reply to your offer. Buy-it-Now sales of one type or another apparently constitute slightly more than half of the total sales on eBay, so it would be wrong to think of eBay purely as an auction site. Vast amounts of new and second-hand goods are sold using the fixed price auction method, or one of its variants.

Getting carried away

I was listening to the radio some time ago when one of the Radio 5 Live presenters stated that she was a typical eBay "newbie", and after opening an account had immediately bought several cars! She then had to explain to the sellers that she did not actually want the cars, and had to rely on their understanding to get her "off the hook". I think that she was not really typical of newcomers to eBay, but there was an element of truth in what she said. There is a temptation to bid on things "left, right, and centre" without thinking things through properly. When you bid on an eBay auction or use a Buy-it-Now option you are entering into a legally binding contract. While it is unlikely that anyone would sue if you failed to go through with the purchase of an item you won on eBay, this is a situation you should never get into in the first place. For one thing, you could soon find yourself banned from eBay if you win items and do not pay for them.

Only bid on something if you are prepared to go ahead and complete the deal at the price you bid. Do not bid on something in haste, look at the listing again later, and then realise you have bid far too much. Before you bid, check that the item is the exact one you required, that you are satisfied with its condition, that it is complete with any vital accessories, and that it is genuinely worth your intended bid price. It would be a mistake not to bid on something because there are one or two vital accessories missing, but you should check that the missing parts can be obtained, and the bid price should be adjusted downwards to allow for the cost and inconvenience of having to obtain them separately.

Remember the postage charge

You may occasionally buy something where it is a practical proposition to go and collect it in person, but in most cases the goods will have to be posted to you. The cost of postage should be deducted from the total price you are prepared to pay, and that is the price you should bid. These days the postage charge is usually quoted in the listing, but if necessary, check the cost with the seller before bidding.

Multiple items

Another classic beginners' mistake is to search for something, find several listings with items that match your requirements, and then place bids on all of them. In this situation it is possible that none of the bids will be successful, or that only one will succeed and that you will buy the item you need. However, there is a likelihood that you will end up winning two or more items, and you will then be expected to go ahead and buy all of them! Failing to do so could get you banned from eBay. Placing bids on several items and then trying to retract bids when you win one of them is not an acceptable way of doing things either. Again, it is a practice that is likely to get you banned from eBay sooner rather than later. The right way of going about things is to place a bid on the auction that will end first. If you are unsuccessful, repeat the process, and keep bidding on the auction that will end soonest until you win the item or admit defeat and give up. At one time there was a facility built into eBay that largely automated this type of bidding process, but it seems to have been withdrawn due to lack of use. There is probably third party software that achieves much the same thing, but I prefer to take personal control of the bidding process. This encourages a more careful and less cavalier approach.

Avoid high postage

Postage rates for the same item vary enormously. Sometimes there are good reasons for this, and the postage for something like a camera with no accessories is likely to be less than for the same camera that comes complete with its original box, instruction manual, software discs, battery, a battery charger, and several leads. Some sellers subsidise the postage cost in the interests of good customer relations, while others charge the full cost of postages and the packaging materials. Others try to make a profit on the postage charges, and in some cases the postage charge is completely "over the top".

One reason for sellers using high postage costs is to avoid paying most of the final listing fee. The seller pays a final listing fee that is a certain percentage of the selling price. The percentage varies, but is usually ten percent for non-business users. Buyers do not pay any eBay fees incidentally. If an item sells for two pounds and the postage charge is fifteen pounds, the final listing fee is very low as it is based on the selling price of two pounds. If an item sells for fifteen pounds and the postage charge is two pounds, the final value fee is relatively high because it is based on the higher selling price of fifteen pounds. The amount received by the seller is the same in both cases, at a total of seventeen pounds.

Postage fraud

Another reason for a high postage charge being used is to deliberately defraud the buyer. In such cases the goods being sold are faulty or of inferior quality. The buyer will probably demand a refund, and in all probability will get one. However, most sellers will only refund the purchase price, and will not pay for any postage costs when an item is returned, regardless of the reason for its return. In the example given previously, the seller would keep the fifteen pound postage charge and refund the two pounds paid for the item. Having paid the return postage plus the original postage charge, the buyer is about seventeen pounds out of pocket. Meanwhile, the seller still has about fifteen pounds minues some Bay costs. In other words, the seller has made nearly fifteen pounds for selling nothing!

eBay has taken some steps to prevent excessive postage charges, but it is practically impossible to eliminate this practice without placing undue restrictions on sellers. It is therefore something that you might encounter from time to time. Anyone indulging in this ploy is at best less than completely honest, and at worst is a fraudster. Experienced eBay users have nothing to do with any items that have clearly excessive postage charges, and you would be well advised to follow the same tenet.

Typical bidding pattern

If you watch how the bidding progresses on a few items you might find that things develop much as you would expect, with bids being made at intervals, and the price steadily building until the closing time and date of the auction is reached. In other words, the bidding proceeds in a similar fashion to a conventional auction. In the early stages there are bids and counter bids from bargain hunters, with the serious bidders only coming in near the end. Everything is at a much slower pace of course, because the auction will typically run for one week, and it cannot last for less than one day. Note that, unlike some other online auctions, eBay auctions are not extended if a bid is placed close to the closing time.

This is a crucial point in explaining why many auctions do not proceed in the manner described above. With very popular items it is quite possible that things will indeed develop in the expected fashion, and the final price might actually be reached well before the auctions end. A more common scenario is that there is very little bidding initially, with most of the bids being placed just before the auction closes. In many cases the serious bids are placed in the last ten seconds or so of the auction! This can be partially explained by people placing a bid on one item, and then moving on to the next item of that type if they do not win the first one. This process of waiting for one item to end before moving on to the next tends to produce late bidding, but it does not really explain the sudden rush of bids in the last few seconds.

Sniping

The rush of bids at the end of many auctions is due to a practice known as "sniping", which is deliberately waiting until the auction is about to close before placing a bid. The main idea of this bidding in the last few seconds is that it does not give your competitors any time to have a change of mind and increase their bid. If you place a bid at the maximum price you are prepared to pay when an auction still has several days to run, it is quite likely that someone will place a bid that is a little lower than your bid. If they place the bid when the auction still has hours or days to run, it is quite possible that they will give in to temptation and place a higher bid before the end of the auction, possibly beating your bid with this second attempt. In fact they might place three or four bids, with a winning bid eventually being placed. This cannot happen if you place your bid about five seconds before the end of the auction. Even if your rival bidder is watching the final stages of the auction and he or she decides to place a higher bid, they will probably not have time to place another bid before the auction ends.

Shill bidding

Sniping also guards against a process known as "shill bidding", or "artificial bidding" as it is also known. This is where the seller uses a second eBay account, or the account of a friend, to place bids on their own auctions. In some cases the idea is to push the bidding up to the price bid by the current highest bidder. One way this is done is to place a high shill bid on the item in order to determine the bid price placed by the victim, and then the bid is retracted. A little later on, a shill bid using a different account is placed just below the victim's maximum bid, taking the current bid price up to that level. More usually, the shill bidding is in the form of numerous bids, with each one moving the price a little higher in an attempt to find the victim's maximum bid price without actually exceeding it.

Sniping is not popular with sellers because, in general, it holds down prices. Also, a seller likes to see steady bidding with the price gradually moving up towards the price they would like to obtain. It is a strain on the nerves if you are selling an item worth about five hundred pounds and the bid price is two pounds and fifty pence with the auction due to close in ten seconds time! However, it is up to buyers to look after their own interests and not those of the seller. Sniping helps to reduce the price paid for eBay items and also reduces the chances of you becoming a victim of shill bidding. It is a legitimate tactic and it makes sense to use it.

Sniping flaw

You do need to be aware of a potential flaw in sniping, which is that the eBay bidding system does not always operate in a fast and efficient manner. Possibly due to high demand on the eBay server, or perhaps due to a bottleneck on the Internet, it can sometimes take a while to place a bid. If you try to place a bid ten seconds from the end of the auction you might fail to get in a bid at all. A temporary blockage in the Internet or a problem with your PC could produce the same result. When bidding on something that is particularly important to you it is probably best to place your bid half a minute or more before the auction closes, rather than leaving it until the last few seconds.

Use PayPal

You might occasionally buy something from someone living close enough for collection in person and payment by cash to be a practical proposition, but most purchases on eBay fall into the "distance selling" category. In other words, you use a method of payment other than cash, and the goods are delivered by the Royal Mail or a courier service. With any form of distance selling there is a risk of the money being paid but no goods being received. With distance selling and buying via eBay the risks can be minimised by using PayPal to pay for purchases. There are additional costs with PayPal transfers, but these are borne by the seller, as are all the eBay fees. Buying items on eBay and using PayPal to pay for them is totally free from fees and surcharges.

PayPal used to be totally separate from eBay, but the company was bought by eBay some years ago and it has to some extent been integrated with the eBay system. You must open a PayPal account in order to make use of this method of sending and receiving money, and your PayPal account can be linked to credit and debit cards and to a bank account. Once you have set up the account it is easy to pay for eBay items that have this payment option. Since it is compulsory for this payment method to be offered when selling most types of goods, it will nearly always be available as a means of payment. You can use PayPal by going through the eBay checkout system, and instant payments can be made from the cards or bank account linked to the PayPal account.

It is a good idea to pay in this way for two main reasons, one of which is simply that it is an instant transfer system, and it avoids having to wait while cheque payments are cleared. There is a version of PayPal payment called an "E-cheque", but it is best to avoid this as far as possible as it is far from instant, and it usually takes about 10-14 days for the payment to clear. The second, and perhaps more important reason for using PayPal, is that you can make a claim from PayPal if the goods are not received, or are significantly different to the description in the listing. This greatly reduces the risk of buying items via eBay. Note that you must use one of the PayNow buttons and go through the ebay/PayPal payment system in order to get this security. Do not pay for eBay items by going through the normal PayPal system for making general payments for goods and services.

Nearly new bargains?

I would guess that most people buying on eBay are looking for bargains, and are trying to obtain goods well below their normal market value. At the most simple level, people are simply looking for second-hand goods at something well below the price of a new equivalent. There are sometimes quite dramatic price differences between nearly new second-hand items and the same thing obtained brand new. There are a couple of points to bear in mind though, and one of these is that the recommended retail prices set by manufacturers are often much higher than a typical shop price. The price from on-line discount sellers can be even lower.

Where appropriate, always check the actual selling prices of new goods before trying to buy them second-hand on eBay or elsewhere. With popular items the differences can be surprisingly small, and you might even find second-hand goods on eBay selling for more than the lowest price for new goods! The difference otherwise tends to be quite high, with a saving of around fifty percent when buying second-hand. The second important point to keep in mind is that second-hand goods do not come complete with a statutory guarantee. The vendor might give some sort of guarantee on the goods, but in most cases they are sold without any form of warranty. You are then taking a chance and gambling that the goods will go on working properly for a reasonable period. It now seems to be the norm for the cost of repairing goods to be higher than their second-hand value, so items that become faulty are often valueless. It is probably not worthwhile buying second-hand unless you can obtain the item at a really good discount to the cost of a new one.

Second chance offers

The eBay system includes a facility whereby a seller can offer items to non-winning bidders. The item offered must either be the one in the listing, or an identical item. Note that you will only receive second chance offers if the appropriate option is selected in your account settings. There can be legitimate reasons for a seller making one or more second chance offers. The most likely reason is that the winning bidder has contacted the seller and made it clear that they will not be completing the sale. If you receive a second chance offer long after the auction ended, it is likely that the winning bidder has not contacted the seller and that the seller has cancelled the sale. Where a seller has several identical items for sale they might list and sell one item, and then offer one or more of the other items to losing bidders who have bid reasonably high amounts. While this might give lower selling prices than auctioning the other items in the normal way, it is relatively quick and easy for the seller, and it also avoids paying additional listing fees. The seller still has to pay the final value fee on second chance offers incidentally.

You need to be a little cautious when receiving second chance offers. There have been various scams in the past that were based on second chance offers. In the main these were based on bogus offers that did not come from the original seller. Changes to the eBay system have to a large extent foiled these scams, but you still have to make sure that any second chance offers are received through the eBay messaging system and not only via the Email account that you use in conjunction with eBay.

Another scam combines second chance offers with shill bidding. The seller places a very high bid on his or her own item, thus ensuring that this is the winning bid. A second chance offer is then made to the bidder with the highest legitimate bid. The point of this is to ensure that the item sells for the highest possible price. It is usually difficult to determine with any certainty whether the winning bid was a legitimate one or a shill bid, and I suppose you might be quite happy to buy the item at your maximum bid price anyway. On the other hand, many buyers prefer to "play safe" and have nothing to do with second chance offers. You have to come to your own decision on this one, but initially at any rate, it is probably best not to take up any second chance offers.

Risky bargains

Many people put a great deal of effort into obtaining real bargains on eBay, and try to obtain goods at a fraction of their normal market value. This can be done, but it is probably much easier for those with a great deal of experience at buying on eBay. Trying to buy the best bargains on eBay is also a bit more risky, and you could end up buying a load of rubbish with little chance of getting your money back. By taking risks that most others are not prepared to take it is possible to obtain massive bargains, but you are likely to waste a certain amount of money as well.

You should end up "well ahead of the game" provided you get things right in the majority of cases.

As a seller, you should get good prices if you put in the effort and list things well. Conversely, you tend to get low prices, and in some cases spectacularly so, if you do not put in the effort and make a mess of things. From the bargain hunter's point of view, it therefore follows that very professionally listed items are unlikely to be a good source of goods at below par prices. In fact the more inept the listing, the better your chances of obtaining a real bargain! The risk is that a listing could be deliberately inept in order to cover up some shortcomings in the item for sale. There might be a possibility of getting a refund through PayPal if the seller is uncooperative and that was the method of payment used. However, it can be difficult to claim that goods were "substantially not as described" if the description is so vague as to be largely meaningless! These are some types of listing to try if you are going to seek out the mega-bargains, and you are prepared to take a risk.

No photograph

Many buyers on eBay will not buy a second-hand item unless there are some reasonable photographs of the item so that they can see what they are buying, and they are in a good position to assess its condition. In particular, those prepared to bid high prices are unlikely to bid on an item unless they can see that it is in good condition. Provided you are prepared to take the risk, this will often leave you to battle it out with the other bargain hunters. Listings that have a stock photograph rather than one of the actual item for sale are equally good targets for bargain hunters. A stock photograph is as much help as no photograph at all!

Terrible photograph

Once again, many potential bidders will have nothing to do with items where they cannot see what they are buying. If you are prepared to take the risk you might get a bargain, but in my experience this is a little riskier than buying items where there are no photographs at all. Sometimes there are one or two general photographs that are quite good, but the close-up shots are very blurred. With small items this is usually the result of the photographer getting the camera too close to the subject, rendering the camera unable to focus properly. Be very suspicious if all the photographs are blurred. Also be very suspicious if they are photographed in a very inept way, such as the item on offer being so small in the photograph that you can barely see it, or a case being carefully positioned so that it largely obliterates your view of the item that goes in it.

Reserve price

On the face of it, bidding should be the same whether or not an item has a reserve price. In reality it does not seem to work this way, and reserve prices often seem to act as a deterrent to bidders. Presumably many potential bidders assume that the reserve price is high and that it is therefore not worth bidding on the item. Anyway, the reserve price might not be particularly high, and you might win if you place a reasonable bid. It is sometimes possible to obtain a bargain with a very modest bid if that bid is the highest one but is still below the reserve price. The seller might decide that your winning bid price is about as much as they are likely to get for the item, and rather than relist it they might send you a second chance offer. It is best to decline if they contact you and try to sell you the item at a figure beyond the winning bid price. Decline any offers to trade outside eBay. Apart from breaking the eBay rules, you obviously lose the normal eBay safeguards if you accept a private deal.

High Buy-it-Now price

High Buy-it-Now prices added to an ordinary auction listing also tend to put people off bidding. Presumably most people see the high Buy-it-Now price and do not bother to investigate any further. If the starting price is quite low it is virtually certain that someone will place a bid before too long. Provided there is no reserve price, the Buy-it-Now option will disappear and the auction will then continue normally. Things are more interesting if the starting price is relatively high, but not unreasonably so. This creates a good chance of the Buy-it-Now staying in place until close to the end of the auction, keeping interest in the item very low. A bid at or just above the starting price might then be successful. The same method can work with any item that has a starting price that is high for a starting price, but would represent a bargain as the final price. It works better when there is also an inflated Buy-it-Now price to deter would-be bidders, but a high starting price on its own is sometimes sufficient to hold down the final price.

Wrong category

A surprising number of items are listed in an inappropriate category. Sometimes it is due to sellers listing an item in two categories. This is encouraged by eBay as it can help sellers to get higher selling prices, and it also increases the fees earned by eBay. The problem is that with many items there is no second category that is really suitable. The secondary listing is unlikely to increase the final selling price, but it is unlikely to decrease it either. It is when an item is only listed in one or more inappropriate categories that things become more interesting. This

Fig.4.1 This grossly underexposed photograph shows little detail

can occur when the seller is lacking in knowledge about the item they are selling, or get careless when listing an item. The eBay system suggests categories when you list an item, and it usually does quite a good job. However, it will usually list some inappropriate categories along with one or two wholly relevant ones. Anyone opting to simply take the first one or two suggestions on the list could easily end up placing the item in categories where it will be seen by few prospective buyers. The lesson here for buyers is to not narrow eBay searches to one or two categories. Searching an entire section of eBay (photography, consumer electronics, etc.) might produce the occasional bargain that would otherwise be missed.

Low feedback

A seller can have a low feedback score simply because they managed to get into a dispute with one buyer, and they have sold few items in the last few months. If they have an exemplary feedback record in other respects they are probably good sellers and a reasonably safe bet. The low feedback score will prevent many people from bidding on their items, which makes them likely candidates for bargains. Even lower prices can be obtained by bidding on items from sellers who have genuinely terrible feedback records, but it is probably best not to do so.

Fig.4.2 The edited image shows a great deal more detail

Photo processing

When a listing includes poor quality photographs it is sometimes possible to process them so that you can see more detail. This will not always be possible, and there is not much that can be done with photographs that are very blurred, only show you the top half of the item for sale, or something of this nature. You can try to adjust an overexposed photograph using a photo-editing program, but it is not usually possible to rescue any worthwhile detail from burned out highlights. The situation is very different with underexposed photographs, where it is often possible to lift a surprising amount of detail from virtually black areas of the picture. Figure 4.1 shows a photograph that is underexposed by at least two stops, but there is still a reasonable amount of detail in the processed version of Figure 4.2. Practically any photo-editing software should have facilities for adjusting the exposure and lightening shadow areas. One slight problem is that the normal Copy and Paste or Save As functions might not work properly when applied to eBay images. An easy way around the problem is to display the large version of a photograph and then operate the Print Screen key to copy the screen to the clipboard. This image can then be pasted onto a blank page in the image editor, where the unwanted parts of the screen can be cropped. The image can then be processed in the normal way.

eBay selling

eBay Selling

Good marketing is all-important when try to sell practically anything, and this is certainly the case when selling your surplus items on eBay. Virtually identical items often sell on eBay at widely differing prices, and I have seen two examples of the same product where one has sold at about ten times the price of the other. The two items were in similar condition, and it was not a case of one being in mint condition and the other being faulty. With auctions there is always a degree of "hit and miss", and two identical items are unlikely to sell at precisely the same price. However, large differences are usually the result of one seller putting in some effort and doing a good job, while the other has not really tried or has simply made a mess of things.

Photographs

Including a photograph of the item for sale is not a requirement of eBay, but few things, if any, will sell well unless the listing features at least one good photograph of the actual item for sale. The first photograph is included in the basic listing fee, but there is a small charge for any further photographs that are used. The eBay system includes stock photographs for a range of popular consumer goods, and they are also available elsewhere. These are mainly intended for those selling new goods, where the item on offer will be as pristine as the one in the photograph. Using stock pictures of new items when selling second-hand goods is not a good idea. When doing so it is essential to make it clear that the photograph is not a picture of the item on offer. People buying second-hand goods want to know the condition of the item for sale, and a stock photograph tells them no more than having no picture at all.

If you do not already have a digital camera it is worth buying a cheap one for eBay use. Photographs on eBay are normally a few hundred pixels on each dimension, although eBay recommend that they should be uploaded at a minimum of about one thousand pixels on the longest dimension. There is the option of paying extra for "Super-Size" pictures, but they are still displayed at a relatively modest size by modern standards. Practically any digital camera can easily handle normal or "Super-Size" pictures, and there is no need for an expensive type that has very high resolution. Something fairly simple should do the job well enough. Note that it is not necessary to upload images at a specific resolution. The eBay system will reduce the pictures to the correct size if you use a higher resolution. If you use a lower resolution the pictures might not be displayed at the maximum size, so this is best avoided.

Camera

A basic digital camera can be obtained quite cheaply these days even if you opt for a new one. A good usable digital camera can be obtained very cheaply second-hand on eBay and from charity shops. Someone recently bet me that I could not obtain a working digital camera for less than five pounds. I eventually obtained a quite sophisticated six megapixel camera for ninety nine pence plus the cost of postage! There are certainly plenty of usable second-hand digital cameras available at around ten pounds plus the cost of postage. However, make sure that the camera comes complete with everything needed in order to use it, or that any extras will be inexpensive, such as a couple of AA batteries. A cheap camera will probably not be a bargain if you have to buy an expensive battery, a charger, and a memory card before you can use it.

Good photographs

According to the old saying "a picture is worth a thousand words", but I think it would probably be more accurate to say that "a *good* picture is worth a thousand words". A bad picture is probably not worth anything, and a mediocre one is perhaps worth a few hundred words. In an eBay context, a bad picture will leave potential buyers none the wiser, and a mediocre one will not be of great help. In both cases there is a risk that potential buyers will think that you are trying to hide something. This can result in them bidding less than they would otherwise be prepared to pay, or simply not bothering to bid at all.

There are two stages in getting really good photographs for your listing, which are to first take at least a reasonably competent photograph, and then to process it to optimise results. Taking bad photographs and then trying to make them good using a photo editing program is not a good approach, and is likely to produce poor to middling results. Try to take photographs that are really good to start with, and then use photo editing software to do some "fine tuning". It is not necessary to spend large amounts of money on a photo editing program. Digital cameras are often supplied complete with basic but reasonably capable editing software, and in some cases the bundled software is actually quite sophisticated. If there is no bundled software that is up to the task it is just a matter of using a free photo editing program such as Google's Picasa or GIMP.

Taking Photographs

To some extent the basic technique for photographing eBay items has to be varied to suit the item concerned. The approach for photographing something sizeable such as a car will inevitably be different to that used when taking the picture of something small such as a gold ring. With a car you can at least wait for a nice day and park it somewhere picturesque so that it is in pleasant looking surroundings. With something like a large electrical appliance or piece of furniture you will probably have to photograph it in situ. You can still tidy up and make the surroundings look as good as possible. Most digital cameras have a zoom lens that covers from a slightly wide angle of view to a moderately telephoto type.

In general, things look better when photographed well back using a telephoto setting rather than at close quarters using a wide angle of view. The problem with the wide-angle approach is that it often results in exaggerated perspective and possibly some odd looking distortions as well. Things tend to look as though they are suffering from "middle-age spread"! Obviously there will not always be sufficient space available to use the longest focal lengths, and it is then a matter of getting as far back as possible and using the longest focal length that enables the complete object to be fitted into the picture.

Avoid backlighting

A common error is to place the subject of the picture on a table directly in front of a window where it will receive plenty of daylight. Getting plenty of light on the subject is definitely a good idea, but with the table directly in front of the window you are inevitably on the opposite side of the table to the light source. In photographic jargon the subject is "backlit", and you are "shooting into the light". Backlighting can be used to good effect in creative ways, but in the current context it is more likely to give a glaring background and a subject that is little more than a silhouette. Results are likely to be better with the subject and the camera the other way around. In other words, you should be close to the window with the light coming from behind you, with the subject on the table which should be placed well into the room.

Avoid camera shake

Another advantage of placing the subject well into the room is that it avoids having it in direct sunlight. While direct sunlight will give a good exposure, it also tends to give harsh shadows and high contrast. The same is true when the light source is a single flashgun. Few things look good with this type of lighting. A more diffuse light source normally gives better results. The main drawback of placing the subject well into the room is that the light level tends to be relatively low. In order to get a proper exposure the shutter speed has to be relatively long, and "camera shake" can then be a problem. In other words, slight movement of the camera during the exposure tends to blur the image, often giving an unpleasant double-image effect.

The best way of avoiding camera shake is to mount the camera on a tripod. Failing that, some cameras have some form of anti-blur facility such as an optical image stabiliser, and using a facility of this type will often provide good results in situations where problems with camera-shake would otherwise occur. With modern cameras it is usually possible to set the sensitivity (ISO) setting quite high, and this gives good shutter speeds even with quite dim lighting. Using a high ISO setting tends to give "noisy" pictures where plain areas of the image have a grainy look. However, in the current context this will probably not be a problem. The grainy look tends to largely disappear when the high definition photographs are reduced to the much lower definition pictures used in the eBay listing.

Using flash

Using the camera's built-in flashgun will normally avoid camera-shake, because the pulse of light from the gun is very brief and it effectively gives a very short shutter time. However, as explained previously, flash lighting tends to be quite harsh and it does not always give particularly good results. Using a flashgun built into the camera often gives problems with the light from the flashgun being reflected back to the camera from shiny surfaces, giving very bright areas and problems with glare. Results are generally better if you can get a reasonable amount of light onto the subject and then use the flashgun as well. A mixture of flash and available light, with the flashgun acting as the main light source, gives much better results than using the flashgun as the sole light source. The natural light softens the shadows and gives a more pleasing result. Flash lighting can also be useful if you cannot avoid having a backlit subject. The light from the flashgun gives a better balance between the subject and the bright background, and should avoid the silhouette problem described previously. This technique is known as "fill-in" flash.

Close-ups (macro)

Items for sale on eBay are often quite small, and while small might be beautiful, for the photographer small is difficult. Most digital cameras have a so-called "macro" mode that enables the camera to focus accurately at much shorter distances than can normally be accommodated. Unfortunately, the macro facility usually operates in a rather unhelpful way, with the greatest macro magnification being possible at the wide-angle end of the lens's zoom range. As explained previously, there can be problems with exaggerated perspective and odd distortions when using a wide-angle lens. These problems tend to be much worse when using a wide-angle lens for close-ups.

Digital zoom

In the current context there is usually an easy way around the problem. Because the camera will be operating at a much higher resolution than that of the final image, it does not matter if the subject is something less than frame-filling in the initial photograph. If the image is cropped to make the subject as large as possible without clipping occurring, it is likely that the resolution of the cropped photograph will still be higher than the minimum needed for an eBay listing. Much the same effect can normally be obtained by using the camera in one of its lower resolution modes and using the digital zoom facility to zoom-in closer. These methods will give much better results than getting too close for the lens to focus properly, or settling for a wide-angle close-up that gives a very distorted and odd looking image.

Fill the frame

Note that it is important to have the subject as large as possible, or something quite close to it. With the modest resolution used for normal eBay pictures, even a frame filling shot will not contain a great deal of detail. With the main subject covering (say) 120 x 180 pixels and a lot of unused background area in the picture, any useful detail might be lost completely. Potential buyers might conclude that you are trying to hide something and they could be put off placing a worthwhile bid.

Keep it clean

It is important that any item you put up for sale on eBay should be free from dust and looking at its best, but it is especially important with small objects. Dust that is not apparent when looking at an object can be very apparent in a close-up photograph. The more close up the photograph, the more obvious any specks of dust are likely to become. Try to get small objects free from dust before starting to photograph them, and if dust is apparent in the photographs, clean the objects and redo the photographs.

Correct focus

The sophisticated electronics in modern cameras has greatly reduced the number of duff photographs due to inaccurate focusing and exposure errors, but it has by no means eliminated them. There are two main causes of pictures being out of focus, and one of these is that the camera cannot focus properly if it is positioned too close to the subject. As pointed out previously, most modern cameras have a macro mode for taking close-up shots, and this facility will often be needed when taking the photographs for eBay listings. Bear in mind that there will still be a limit on how close you can go while still obtaining sharp results.

The other main cause of problems is that the auto-focusing of a camera needs some fine detail with reasonable contrast in order to work properly. This can cause problems when photographing something that has plain surfaces. Some cameras will not actually allow a photograph to be taken unless the auto-focusing has found something it can latch onto, but others will carry on regardless and produce fuzzy pictures. However, there will usually be some form of indicator that lets you know a problem has occurred. Where a camera has the option of using a small area in the middle of the frame, or a much larger area, using this second option increases the chances of the auto-focusing finding something to focus on.

If your camera can only use the centre of the frame for auto-focusing there is a simply ploy that will usually give good results. With most digital cameras the focusing is activated by pressing the shutter button half way down. It is then locked at that setting until the button is fully depressed and the picture is taken. You can therefore get the camera to focus properly by placing any suitable part of the subject at the centre of the frame, pressing the shutter button half way down, waiting for the auto-focusing to operate, framing the subject, and then pressing the shutter all the way down.

Correct exposure

Obtaining accurate exposures is not usually too difficult, and the auto-exposure systems of modern cameras can handle most situations. However, there are some circumstances that can cause problems.

Objects that are very light in colour can "fool" automatic exposure systems into producing under exposure, and rather dark pictures. Conversely, very dark objects can come out far too light in the pictures due to over exposure. It is possible to compensate for small amounts of over and under exposure using a photo editing program, but results are generally best if you get things right at the taking stage.

Most cameras have an exposure compensation facility that can be used to correct the exposure in awkward situations where exposure problems will otherwise occur. Use positive exposure compensation to make pictures lighter, or the negative variety to make them darker. With black objects, or those that are very dark in colour, it can be advantageous to use a small amount of over exposure. With a technically correct exposure you can end up with a picture of a black blob that is not recognisable as anything at all! A small amount of over exposure can bring out some detail in the picture and produce something that is a better representation of the object. Only use a small amount of overexposure though, or you could end up with a photograph that makes the object look a bit battered and worn.

Shoot at an angle

Using the camera's built-in flashgun is a common cause of under exposure. Shiny surfaces tend to reflect the light from the flashgun back to the camera, and these very bright highlights "fool" the automatic exposure system into producing under exposure. In an extreme case you end up with a picture that is white in the highlight areas but is otherwise black. Photographing objects at an angle rather than square-on will usually eliminate large reflections, and may well give a better composed photograph as well. Most cameras have an exposure compensation facility that will work when using the built-in flashgun, but this may be separate from the normal exposure compensation facility.

How many pictures?

The first picture in a listing is included free, but a small additional fee has to be paid for any further pictures. Note that this fee is doubled if an item is listed in two categories. The cost of including extra photographs is minimal compared to the value of expensive items, but with very low cost items you could potentially pay more in fees than you would actually receive from the sale! Also, with some things you can give potential buyers a much better idea of what the item looks like by using half a dozen or more photographs, while one or two photographs can be perfectly adequate with other items. A little common sense has to be exercised here. With something that is fairly expensive and looks quite impressive it could be worthwhile paying extra for using "Super-Size" images.

Try to avoid including, and paying for, superfluous photographs. I have seen many eBay listings where several photographs of a group of objects have been provided, but all the photographs were general shots of the group that looked much the same. There is no point in using additional photographs that provide no more information than the first one. With an auction lot that consists of a main item plus some accessories it is a good idea to include a general shot that shows everything that is up for sale. Try to group the objects very close together so that each one is reasonably large in the photograph. However, it is still a good idea to include one or two shots showing the main item in more detail. For example, with a camera you could use a general shot showing the camera together with any included accessories such as the battery charger and instruction manual. Close-up shots showing front and rear views of just the camera would then be added to show potential buyers the condition of the main item.

Processing

Having obtained some good photographs of the items for sale it is likely that most of the pictures would benefit from a certain amount of processing to optimise results. There is insufficient space available here for a detailed description of all the processes involved in picture optimisation, but in most cases a few simple types of processing will suffice. It may be possible to apply some or even all of the processing in-camera, but it will usually be necessary to use an image editing program. As explained previously, a basic but adequate program of this type is often included with digital cameras, or a free image editing program such as GIMP or Google's Picasa can be downloaded from the Internet.

Cropping

The importance of frame-filling shots to maximise the available resolution was pointed out previously. Even if you frame the shot well, leaving just a small amount of unused background area, it is likely that main subject will shrink and that there will be substantially more background in evidence when the picture is displayed on a computer. The reason for this is that the viewfinders of cameras, whether optical or electronic, are often designed to show only about 85 to 90 percent of the picture. The main reason for this is that one of the most common errors when taking pictures is to frame the shot too tightly so that important details are lost outside the margins of the photograph. The classic example of this is where someone takes a picture of a group of people, only to discover that the tops of peoples' heads are absent when the picture is printed.

One way around the problem is to deliberately frame shots a little too tightly in the viewfinder so that the full image is framed correctly. However, this tends to be a bit "hit and miss", and it is usually better to compose the picture normally in the viewfinder and then crop it later. Some cameras have the ability to crop pictures, but it is a task that can be handled more accurately and easily using photo-editing software. Any picture processing software should have a facility that enables images to be accurately cropped.

Exposure adjustment

If there are major problems with the incorrect exposure it is better to retake the shot using a suitably adjusted exposure, rather than trying to rescue a grossly underexposed or overexposed photograph. It might be worthwhile trying to adjust the image if it is only suffering from minor overexposure, but with anything more than that it is likely that detail will be lost in the highlights. Slight underexposure is not usually a serious problem, and the automatic exposure systems of many digital cameras are deliberately designed to err on the side of underexposure. The reasoning behind this is that even mild overexposure tends to cause a loss of detail in the highlights, whereas shadow detail can usually be rescued when there is slight underexposure.

The way in which adjustments to the brightness, exposure, and contrast are handled depends on the photo-editing software in use. Some cameras have an image optimisation facility, as do most photo-editing programs in one form or another. There will often be automated features for adjusting individual aspects of an image, such as contrast, exposure, and colour balance. It makes sense to use automated features with images where they work well, but there will inevitably be a fair percentage of photographs where they have little effect or even make things worse. You then have to use the manual alternatives and exercise your own judgement. In general it is best to use no more processing of images than is really necessary.

Resizing

The resolution of the images produced by a modern digital camera, even after a certain amount of cropping, will usually be far higher than the normal size used in eBay listings. As explained previously, eBay recommends uploading oversize images at about one thousand pixels or so on the longest dimension. This is still well below the sizes produced by a reasonably modern digital camera. It is not essential to resize your eBay pictures to match these limits, since the eBay system will automatically reduce images to the required size. However, it can be advantageous to do so, and practically every image editing program has a resizing facility. One advantage of reducing the size of pictures is that it reduces the time taken to upload them to the eBay server. This is especially important if you are using a slow Internet connection such as an ordinary dial-up type. There is also something to be said for reducing the pictures to the appropriate size before carrying out any processing. You will be seeing the photographs more or less as they will appear on the screen when potential buyers view them. Any processing applied should be apposite to the final image. Processing that looks fine on a large image will not necessarily look quite so good once it has been reduced to a much smaller size. Any sharpening should only be added once any other processing has been completed and the image has been reduced to its final size. Use sharpening in moderation as it can exaggerate any slightly imperfections in the subject matter.

Sections

eBay is divided into various sections and subsections in order to make it easier for buyers to find the type of goods they require. When selling an item it is necessary to specify the section that it will appear in. Some items are appropriate for two sections, and in such cases the same listing can be placed in two sections. For example, a camera lens for a modern digital camera might also fit some film cameras as well, and listing it in both the appropriate sections would increase the chances of obtaining a high selling price. An item cannot be listed in more than two sections, and note that listing in two sections results in all the listing fees being doubled. There is still only one final value fee to pay though.

Heading

Some eBay sellers fail to realise the importance of suitable wording in the headings for listings, which tends to be a costly mistake. A heading such as "camera" or "car" is unlikely to bring in dozens of bidders. Most people on seeing a heading such as this will not bother to investigate further. Those that do bother to look at the listing will probably be professional eBay users or experienced amateur users looking to buy things at a fraction of their true value. Most of your potential buyers will never know that your item exists because they will use the eBay search engine to locate items, and a vague description in the heading is unlikely to match their search terms.

It is generally considered better to use a long heading because this makes your listing larger and more obvious in a list of search results. It also means that you can use plenty of words in the heading, thus increasing your chances of matching the search terms used by people using the eBay search engine.

A good way of going about things is to write down any search terms that you might use if you were looking for an item like the one you have for sale. Try to use all of them, or failing that as many as possible of them, in the heading. Make sure that any really important search criteria are included. With an ornament for example, it will probably have a maker, a name for that particular piece, and possibly some form of maker's number such as a catalogue number. Ideally these should all be included in the heading, and they should certainly be included in the main text of the listing.

If an object is in particularly fine condition it is probably best to indicate this in the heading. If it is in bad condition it is not really necessary to mention this fact in the heading, but it should obviously be made clear in the description. If it is faulty then this should definitely be indicated in the heading. eBay now has more than just "new" and "used" options in the Condition menu when listing items, and there is one specifically for faulty items. Make sure that you use this one where appropriate, and not the "used" one.

Description

Do include a proper description, and do not simply leave this blank or use something so vague that it is of no real use to potential buyers. Make sure that potential buyers know exactly what you have on offer. Where appropriate state the colour, size, or whatever. Size is especially important with items that are made in more than one size, and this does not just apply to clothes. Numerous products, including ornaments, toys, and camera bags are often produced in more than one size. With some items there is no way potential customers can know the size unless you give dimensions in the description. If you do not specify the size there is a risk that your customer will jump to conclusions. There will be trouble if your customer expects to receive a vase that is half a metre high and they receive one the size of a thimble!

Try to give a description that will give people a good idea of an item's condition. Try to be honest and give an accurate description. Do not "gloss over" or omit any mention of bad points, but it is also a mistake to list lots of tiny imperfections. This will make the item sound much worse that it is, and will deter potential bidders. A more vague description is acceptable and is all that most potential bidders require. Something along the lines of "it has some general wear, mainly on the back, in the form of a few superficial scratches" is all that is needed.

Any significant damage should be mentioned, and should preferably be visible in one of the photographs as well. Be careful with the wording. If something can be described as "almost perfect" if it is in fantastic condition apart from a tiny scratch. It could also be described as "slightly damaged". The first description should bring in plenty of bidders whereas the second one is likely to put people off bidding at all. The difference in the price obtained could be massive. It is a matter of trying to emphasise the good rather than the bad, while not going so far as to be misleading. If an item is rare or unusual in some way, make sure that this is mentioned in the description. Mention anything that makes the item more desirable and valuable than most other objects of that type.

Starting price

If you opt to sell an item using a straightforward auction it is not necessary to set a price for your item. The bidders will determine the final price, although you still have to set the starting price. It is not possible to set a reserve price of less than fifty pounds, which is clearly an unrealistically high level for many of the items sold on eBay. However, it is possible to set the starting price anywhere from a few pence to many thousands of pounds, making it possible to use the starting price as a sort of pseudo reserve figure on an item.

It is only fair to point out that using a high starting price is not necessarily a good way of doing things. If you have watched auction programmes on the television you will probably be well aware that some items sell for much more than expected, while others do quite badly and in some cases do not even attract a single bid. While using a high starting price does ensure that you do not end up selling the item for next to nothing, it can also have the effect of deterring would-be bidders. Using a low starting price together with a reserve often seems to produce the same result, with many bidders being put off and not bothering to place bids.

Using a low start

A very low starting price of 99 pence is usually the best approach with popular items that are in demand. Higher starting prices cost more, so a 99 pence start helps to minimise your listing fees. A low starting price also attracts bidders, with the bargain hunters bidding early and the serious bidders coming in towards the end. This can give an auction a sort of momentum, and a low starting price usually gives better results than a high initial price. eBay used to offer free listing days on auctions starting at 99 pence or less in an attempt to encourage people to use this way of doing things. eBay has now taken this idea a step further, and these days most auctions starting at 99 pence or less have a basic listing fee that is free.

A low starting price is not always a good idea, and it can be disastrous with less popular items. You will end up selling your item for 99 pence if there are only two bidders interested in it and one of them forgets to bid! There are two ways of avoiding a disastrously low selling price, and one is to set a starting price equal to the lowest price at which you would be reasonably happy to sell the item. The other is to not use an auction format listing at all, but to use a Buy-it-Now type instead. In other words, use a listing that is effectively a straightforward second-hand advertisement where you set a selling price. Either way there is a risk that the item will not sell, but this is better than selling a rare and valuable item for a few pounds or for a matter of pence. If the pricing is fair, items that do not sell at the first attempt will often do so if they are relisted. There is normally only one listing fee to pay if a relisted item sells at the second attempt, but there are some exceptions.

Variations

There are variations on these two approaches, including one that combines the two, with a fairly high starting price being used together with a Buy-it-Now option at a slightly higher price. Do not bother trying to combine a low starting price with a high Buy-it-Now price. The Buy-it-Now option disappears when the first bid is placed, or when the reserve price is met in the case of an auction that has a reserve in place. If you use a low starting price and no reserve there will always be a joker who places an early and very low bid. This seems to be pure mischief making and is done to specifically to remove the Buy-it-Now option. There is usually no intention to make a serious bid at a later time.

This is one situation where a reserve can be used to good effect, as it can protect the Buy-it-Now option from mischievous bidders. However, bear in mind that there is a 50 pound minimum for a reserve value. Also, unlike most other types of auction, there is an extra charge for using a reserve on an eBay auction, and this adds significantly to the cost of the listing. There is an advantage in using a reserve, which is that it acts as a sort of pseudo bidder with a bid just below the reserve price. Anyone placing a bid at or above the reserve price will become the highest bidder at the reserve price. They will win the item at that price if no other bids are placed. Normally you need two obliging bidders in order to obtain a high price, but this is not the case when a reserve is used, with the reserve effectively acting as an initial high bidder. Despite this potential advantage it is generally best to avoid using reserves, which tend to be an expensive way of putting off would-be bidders.

The right price

It is important to be realistic when setting a Buy-it-Now or high auction starting price. If you set the price too high it is possible that you will get lucky and someone will be mug enough to buy it at that price, but it is more likely that you will end up spending a lot of money listing and relisting the item. You need to avoid making the opposite mistake where something is listed using the Buy-it-Now option, and sells within about 30 seconds because you have set the price way below the true value of the item. Anything you sell on eBay, or anywhere else, is worth what someone will pay for it, and not what you would like them to pay for it. Setting fanciful prices on things is folly, and selling things at a fraction of their true market value is plain daft.

Do not get conned

Although most people probably consider it is buyers on eBay that are most at risk from various scams, with the current eBay system there is very little risk for buyers of most goods provided they pay using PayPal and go through the official eBay channels. The situation is similar for sellers if payment is made via PayPal, and many sellers will now only accept payment via PayPal. If you accept some other form of payment it is important to ensure that it has fully cleared before you part with the goods. Cash on collection might seem to be safe enough, but using counterfeit money to buy second-hand goods is a common way for crooks to unload their dodgy money. It is better to insist on payment by cheque or PayPal in advance, and to only allow collection of the goods once payment has cleared.

Offers

When you list something on eBay, particularly if it has a low starting price, you will almost certainly receive either offers to buy it immediately, or requests for a Buy-it-Now price. The people making these offers will sometimes come up with supposedly good reasons why they cannot wait until the end of the auction, such as they will shortly be going away on holiday. The vast majority of these messages are from people trying to buy the item at a fraction of its true value, which is why you should ignore them and let the auction run its course. Never be enticed into dealing outside eBay by one of these messages.

6

Security

From all sides

Computer security has been a growth industry in recent years, with ever more ways of protecting PCs being devised in response to increasingly imaginative ways of attacking them. Viruses are the best known form of computer attack, but there are other ways that hackers can mount an assault on your PC. In fact many of the much publicised computer viruses are not, strictly speaking, viruses at all. The non-technical press tend to call any form of software that attacks computers a virus. A virus is a specific type of program though, and represents just one of several types that can attack a computer. Initially, someone attaches the virus to a piece of software, and then finds a way of getting that software into computer systems. These days the Internet is the most likely route for the infection to be spread, but it is important not to overlook the fact that there are other means of propagating viruses. Indeed, computer viruses were being spread around the world long before the Internet came along.

Programs and possibly other files can carry viruses regardless of the source. If someone gives you a floppy disc, CD-ROM, or DVD containing software it is possible that the contents of the disc are infected with a virus. In the early days of personal computing the main route for viruses to spread was by way of discs containing illegally copied programs. Discs containing pirated software are still used to propagate viruses. Avoid any dodgy software if you wish to keep your PC virus-free.

Boot sector

Anyway, having introduced a virus into a system via one route or another, it will attack that system and try to replicate itself. Some viruses only attack the boot sector of a system disc. This is the part of the disc that the computer uses to boot into the operating system. Other viruses will try to attach themselves to any file of the appropriate type, which usually means a program file of some sort. The attraction of a program file is that the user will probably run the program before too long, which gives the virus a chance to spread the infection and (or) to start attacking the computer system. At one time there were only two possible ways in which a virus could attack a computer. One way was for the virus to attach itself to a program file that the user then ran on his or her computer.

The other was for someone to leave an infected floppy disc in the computer when it was switched off. On switching the computer on again the floppy disc was used as the boot disc, activating the virus in the disc's boot sector.

Script virus

These days you have to be suspicious of many more types of file. Many applications programs such as word processors and spreadsheets have the ability to automate tasks using scripts or macros as they are also known. The application effectively has a built-in programming language and the script or macro is a form of program. This makes it possible for viruses or other harmful programs to be present in many types of data file. Scripts are also used in some web pages, and viruses can be hidden in these JavaScript programs, Java applets, etc. There are other potential sources of infection such as Email attachments. I would not wish to give the impression that all files, web pages, and Emails are potential sources of script or macro viruses. There are some types of file where there is no obvious way for them to carry a virus or other harmful program. A simple text file for example, should be completely harmless. Even in cases where a harmful program is disguised as a text file with a "txt" extension, the file should be harmless. The system will treat it as a text file and it can not be run provided no one alters the file extension. Similarly, an Email that contains a plain text message can not contain a script virus. Nevertheless, it is probably best to regard all files and Emails with a degree of suspicion. As explained later in this chapter, even though simple text can not carry a true virus, it can carry a virus of sorts.

Benign virus

It tends to be assumed that all viruses try to harm the infected computer system. This is not correct though, and many viruses actually do very little. For example, you might find that nothing more occurs than a daft message appears onscreen when a certain date is reached, or on a particular date each year. Viruses such as this certainly have a degree of nuisance value, but they are not harmful. I would not wish to give the impression that most viruses are harmless. Many computer viruses do indeed try to do serious damage to the infected system. If in doubt you have to assume that a virus is harmful.

Worm

A worm is a program that replicates itself, usually from one disc to another, or from one system to another via a local network or the Internet. Like a virus, a worm is not necessarily harmful. In recent times many of the worldwide virus scares have actually been caused by worms transmitted via Email, and not by what would normally be accepted as a virus. The usual ploy is for the worm to send a copy of itself to every address in the Email address book of the infected system. A worm spread in this way, even if it is not intrinsically harmful, can have serious consequences. There can be a sudden upsurge in the amount of Email traffic, possibly causing parts of the Email system to seriously slow down or even crash. Some worms compromise the security of the infected system, perhaps enabling it to be used by a hacker for sending spam for example.

Trojan horse

A Trojan horse, or just plain Trojan as it is now often called, is a program that is supposed to be one thing but is actually another. In the early days many Trojans were in the form of free software, and in particular, free antivirus programs. The users obtained nasty shocks when the programs were run, with their computer systems being attacked. Like viruses, some Trojans do nothing more than display stupid messages, but others attack the disc files, damage the boot sector of the hard disc, and so on.

Backdoor Trojan

A backdoor Trojan is the same as the standard variety in that it is supplied in the form of a program that is supposed to be one thing but is actually another. In some cases nothing appears to happen when you install the program. In other cases the program might actually install and run as expected. In both cases one or two small programs will have been installed on the computer and set to run when the computer is booted.

One ploy is to have programs that produce log files showing which programs you have run and Internet sites that you have visited. The log will usually include any key presses as well. The idea is for the log file to provide passwords to things such as your Email account, online bank account, and so on. Someone hacking into your computer system will usually look for the log files, and could obviously gain access to important information from these files. Another ploy is to have a program that makes it easier for hackers to break into your computer system. A backdoor Trojan does not attack the infected computer in the same way as some viruses, and it does not try to spread the infection to other discs or computers. Potentially though, a backdoor Trojan is more serious than a virus, particularly if you use the computer for online banking, share dealing, etc. This is currently one of the most common types of computer malware.

Spyware

Spyware programs monitor system activity and send information to another computer by way of the Internet. There are really two types of spyware, and one of them tries to obtain passwords and send them to another computer. This takes things a step further than the backdoor Trojan programs mentioned earlier. A backdoor Trojan makes it easier for a hacker to obtain sensitive information from your PC, but it does not go as far as sending any information that is placed in the log files. Spyware is usually hidden in other software in Trojan fashion.

Adware

The second type of spyware is more correctly called adware. In common with spyware, it gathers information and sends it to another computer via the Internet. Adware is not designed to steal passwords or other security information from your PC. Its purpose is usually to gather information for marketing purposes, and this typically means gathering and sending details of the web sites you have visited. Some free programs are supported by banner advertising, and the adware is used to select advertisements that are likely to be of interest to you. Programs that are supported by adware have not always made this fact clear during the installation process. Sometimes the use of adware was pointed out in the End User License Agreement, but probably few people bother to read the "fine print". These days the more respectable software companies that use this method of raising advertising revenues make it clear that the adware will be installed together with the main program. There is often the option of buying a "clean" copy of the program. Others try to con you into installing the adware by using the normal tricks.

Dialers

A dialer is a program that uses a modem and an ordinary dial-up connection to connect your PC to another computer system. Dialers probably have numerous legitimate applications, but they are mainly associated with various types of scam. An early one was a promise of free pornographic material that required a special program to be downloaded. This program was, of course, the dialer, which proceeded to call a high cost number in a country thousands of miles away. In due course the user received an astronomic telephone bill. A modern variation on this is where users are tricked into downloading a dialer, often with the promise of free software of some description. The user goes onto the Internet in the usual way via their dial-up connections, and everything might appear to be perfectly normal. What is actually happening though is that they are not connecting to the Internet via their normal Internet service provider (ISP). Instead, the dialer is connecting them to a different ISP that is probably thousands of miles away and is costing a fortune in telephone charges. Again, the problem is very apparent when the telephone bill arrives.

The increasing use of broadband Internet connections has removed the threat of dialer related problems for many, but users of dial-up connections still need to guard against this problem

Hoax virus

A hoax virus might sound innocuous enough and just a bit of a joke, but it has the potential to spread across the world causing damage to computer systems. The hoax is usually received in the form of an Email from someone that has contacted you previously. They say that the Email they sent you previously was infected with a virus, and the Email then goes on to provide information on how to remove the virus. This usually entails searching for one or more files on your PC's hard disc drive and erasing them. Of course, there was no virus in the initial Email. The person that sent the initial Email could be the hoaxer, or they might have been fooled by the hoax themselves. The hoax Email suggests that you contact everyone that you have emailed recently, telling them that their computer could be infected and giving them the instructions for the "cure". This is the main way in which a hoax virus is propagated. The files that you are instructed to remove could be of no real consequence, or they could be important system files. It is best not to fall for the hoax and find out which!

These hoax viruses demonstrate the point that all the antivirus software in the world will not provide full protection for your PC. They are simple text files that do not do any direct harm to your PC, and can not be kept at bay by software. Ultimately it is up to you to use some common sense and provide the final line of defence. A quick check on the Internet will usually provide details of hoax viruses and prevent you from doing anything silly.

Phishing

There are other scams that involve hoax emails, and there have been numerous instances of fake Emails being sent to customers of online financial companies. These purport to come from the company concerned, and they ask customers to provide their passwords and other account details. A link is provided to the site, and the site usually looks quite convincing. It is not the real thing though, and anyone falling for it has their account details stolen. These are called "phishing" attacks, and many millions of pounds have now been stolen in this way. The best defence against phishing attacks is to always go to financial sites via your normal route, such as typing the URL into the address bar or using an option in the favourites menu. Never use links provided in Emails.

Basic measures

The obvious way of protecting a PC from viruses and other harmful programs is to simply keep it away from possible sources of infection. Unfortunately, the quarantine approach is not usually a practical one. Little real world computing is compatible with this standalone approach. I use my PC to produce letters that are sent through the post, but I probably send about 100 times as many Emails, and receive about 100 Emails for every "snail mail" letter. I also receive data discs occasionally, and these have to be read using my computer. I have to use the Internet extensively for research, and I sometimes download software updates. Isolating my computer from the outside world would render it largely useless to me. Totally removing the threat of attack is not usually possible, but the chances of a successful attack can be greatly reduced by using a few basic precautions.

Email attachments

Some individuals operate a policy of never opening Email attachments. I do not take things that far, but I would certainly not open an Email attachment unless I knew the sender of the Email and was expecting the attachment. Bear in mind that some viruses and worms spread by hijacking a user's Email address book and sending copies of the infected Email to every address in the address book. The fact that an Email comes from someone you know, or purports to, does not guarantee that it is free from infection. Another point to bear in mind is that Email attachments are now the most common way of spreading viruses and computer worms. Never activate a link in an Email unless you are sure that it is genuine and from a trustworthy source. The link might take your browser to a site that will attempt to attack your PC.

Selective downloading

Downloading software updates from the main computer software companies should be safe, as should downloading the popular freebies from their official sources. Downloading just about anything else involves a degree of risk and should be kept to a minimum. Never download and install any program unless you are sure that it is from a reliable source.

Pirate software

Pirated software has become a major problem for the software companies in recent years. In addition to casual software piracy where friends swap copies of programs there is now an epidemic of commercial copying. Apart from the fact that it is illegal to buy and use pirate software, unlike the real thing, some of it contains viruses, spyware, etc. A substantial percentage of the pirate software available for download on the Internet contains Trojans, viruses, or other malware.

Built-in protection

Some programs, and particularly those from Microsoft, have built-in virus protection that is designed to block known macro/script viruses. If you have any programs that include this feature, make sure that it is enabled. Similarly, browsers often have one or more protection measures. Features such as these do not guarantee that your computer will be free from attacks and a certain amount of common sense has to be exercised, but it makes sense to use any built-in security measures that are available.

P2P

P2P (peer to peer) programs are widely used for file swapping. Even if you use this type of software for swapping legal (non-pirated) files, it still has to be regarded as very risky. In most cases you have no idea who is supplying the files, or whether they are what they are supposed to be. Also, you are providing others with access to your PC, and this access could be exploited by hackers.

Switch off

Some PC users leave their computers running continuously in the belief that it gives better reliability. It did in the days when computers were based on valves, but there is no evidence that it improves reliability with modern computers. It will increase your electricity bills, and it also increases the vulnerability of your PC if it has some form of always-on Internet connection. No one can hack into your computer system if it is switched off.

Prevention

The old adage about "prevention is better than cure" certainly applies to computer viruses. In addition to some basic security precautions, equip

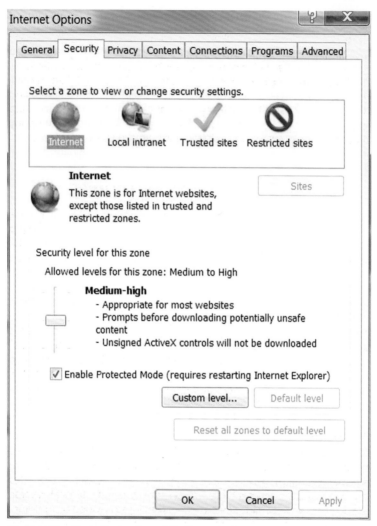

Fig.6.1 The Security section of the Internet Options window

your PC with antivirus software and keep it up-to-date. This software will usually detect and deal with viruses before they have a chance to spread the infection or do any damage to your files.

Backup

Always have at least one backup copy of any important data file. This is not just a matter of having a replacement copy if a file should be destroyed by a virus. The hard disc of a computer has a finite lifespan, and hard disc failures are not a rarity. You should backup all important data anyway, just in case there is a major hard disc failure. It is a good idea to backup the entire system from time to time. This makes it easy to restore a working version of the system, applications programs, etc., in the event of any major problem such as a virus attack, corrupted Windows installation, or hard disc failure.

IE settings

In order to make a PC really secure when using the Internet it is necessary to have some hardware and (or) software to protect the system. However, you can improve security by using the computer in the correct manner when online and by having the best settings in Internet Explorer. The settings can be changed by selecting Internet Options from the Tools menu, and then operating the Security tab in the new window that appears (Figure 6.1). The easy way to alter the level of security is to use the slider control near the middle of the window. The higher the setting of this control, the greater the security provided. However, the level of security is increased by disabling various automatic features. With these features disabled it is not possible for an attack site to exploit them, but neither can a site that would make legitimate use of these facilities. Therefore, a high setting will give excellent security, but you will probably find that some web sites no longer work properly with Internet Explorer. You have to use trial and error to find the highest setting that does not prevent Internet Explorer from working acceptably with the web sites that you use frequently.

Of course, it is possible to use one setting for normal Internet use, and a higher one when surfing the Internet and visiting web sites of unknown legitimacy. Changing from one setting to another is quick and easy. No reboot is required, and neither is it necessary to restart Internet Explorer. You do not have to use the preset security settings provided by the slider control, and operating the Custom Level button produces a new window where it is possible to individually enable or disable each function (Figure 6.2).

Phishing filter

Some browsers now have a phishing filter, which is a feature that blocks access and warns you if the selected web page is part of a known phishing

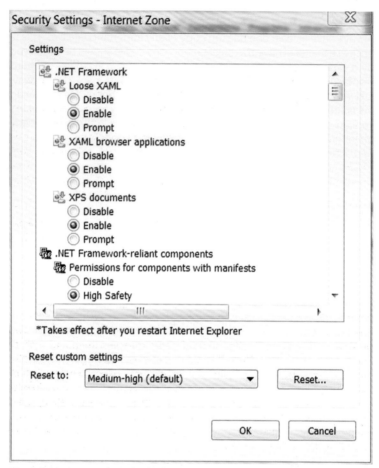

Fig.6.2 You can select the individual facilities that will be disabled

site. It would be a mistake to rely totally on a feature such as this, since it can only warn you about sites that have been reported and found to be genuine fakes. It will not block phishing sites that are very new and have not yet been reported and checked. You still have to use some common sense and try to spot phishing sites yourself. However, it is clearly a good idea to use any feature of this type, which might prevent you from doing something silly. It is also a good idea to make use of any other feature that blocks the browser from entering other forms of malicious web site.

Mystery files

Be very careful if you find a file on your PC and you do not know what it is or how it found its way onto the hard disc. Opening some form of document file (PDF, DOC, and so on) or running some form of program file (EXE or COM) could activate some form of attack. Simply deleting a mystery file is not a good idea because it might be a file you need but have forgotten about. It is better to first copy the file to a floppy disc, CD/RW, Flash memory card, or whatever, and then delete the original. The normal Delete function of Windows puts erased files in the Recycle Bin rather than deleting them straight away. This could leave a Trojan or similar file still on the hard disc. In order to genuinely delete a file it is first selected using Windows Explorer, and then the Delete key is pressed while holding down the Shift key. The file will appear to have been deleted in the normal way, but it will be conspicuously absent from the Recycle Bin.

Keep up-to-date

Many viruses and worms are designed to exploit a security flaw in an applications program or the operating system itself. Sometimes these flaws have already been covered by software updates, but not everyone has bothered to update their PCs and the infection is able to spread. In fairness to amateur PC users, there have been worms that have exploited old security "holes" in the operating systems of servers. The professionals maintaining the affected servers had not bothered to routinely update their systems. Some worms and viruses exploit previously unknown security flaws, but patches to fix the problem are soon made available when this sort of thing occurs.

Some applications programs now have an automatic update facility, as does the Windows operating system. A system such as this could be regarded as a potential security risk itself, but manual updates are usually available from the software publisher's web site if you do not trust the automatic approach.

Firewalls

Although some people seem to think that a firewall and antivirus programs are the same, there are major differences between the two. There is often some overlap between real world antivirus and firewall programs, but their primary aims are completely different. An antivirus program is designed to scan files on discs and the contents of the computer's memory in search of viruses and other potentially harmful files. Having found any suspect files, the program will usually deal with them. A firewall is used to block access to your PC, and in most cases it is access to your PC via the Internet that is blocked. Bear in mind though, that a software firewall will usually block access via a local area network (LAN) as well. Of course, a firewall is of no practical value if it blocks communication from one PC to another and access via the Internet. What it is actually doing is keeping hackers at bay by preventing unauthorised access to the protected PC. When you access an Internet site your PC sends messages to the server hosting that site, and these messages request the pages you wish to view. Having requested information, the PC expects information to be sent from the appropriate server, and it accepts that information when it is received. A firewall does not interfere with this type of Internet activity provided it is set up correctly.

Blocking access

It is a different matter when another system tries to access your PC when you have not instigated the initial contact. The firewall will treat this attempted entry as an attack and will block it. Of course, the attempt at accessing your PC might not be an attack, and a firewall can result in legitimate access being blocked. Something like P2P file swapping is likely to fail or operate in a limited fashion. The sharing of files and resources on a local area network could also be blocked. A practical firewall enables the user to permit certain types of access so that the computer can work normally while most unauthorised access is still blocked. However, doing so does reduce the degree of protection provided by the firewall. Recent versions of Windows come complete with a basic firewall program that is enabled by default. There are plenty of commercial firewall programs that can be used instead if you feel that a more sophisticated Firewall program would be desirable. Note some broadband routers have a built-in firewall, but the capabilities of these facilities vary considerably.

Digital certificates

Digital certificates are something that you are likely to encounter on the Internet from time to time. The purpose of the certificate is to guarantee the identity of an individual or organisation, and they could be regarded as the digital version of a passport. Having the identity of the person or organisation properly verified should in turn guarantee that you can safely download their program, use their site, or whatever. Typically a digital certificate is encountered when downloading a player program to permit a media file to be played. Digital certificates are also much used for secure web sites.

In order to be of any value the certificate must be issued by a recognised certificate authority (CA) such as VeriSign. Certificates have an expiry date and must be renewed from time to time. Occasionally a warning message might be produced as you enter a site, due to the certificate having been allowed to lapse. There is probably nothing to worry about if the site is one that is tried and tested. The certificate has probably been allowed to lapse due to an oversight. If the site is not one that you have used regularly in the past it is probably a good idea to give it a miss until the certificate is renewed.

Secure site?

Many web sites claim that they are secure and that any information that you supply to them is hacker-proof, but how do you know if a site is actually a secure type? For that matter, what exactly is a secure site? Sites that take sensitive information such as credit card details normally use encryption so that your information is safe from hackers. A hacker might actually intercept the information, but as it is encrypted it is not in a form that is of any use to them. Even using the most powerful computers available today it would take many years to "crack" the code and extract your credit card details, or whatever. No one is going to bother, and the information would probably be well out of date by the time it was recovered by a hacker.

By default, Internet Explorer will tell you when you are entering and leaving a secure site. This can get a bit irritating, so most users switch off these messages. Even where they are still operational, it can be difficult to keep track of things if the messages keep popping up. Fortunately it is very easy to determine whether or not a secure site is being accessed using Internet Explorer. A tiny padlock icon appears near the bottom right-hand corner of the window when visiting a secure site using one of the older versions of Internet Explorer. If this icon is absent, the site is not secure, even it contains claims to the contrary. With later versions the address bar goes green when visiting a secure site. Again, the site is not a secure type if this fails to happen. Most other browsers use a similar system.

Online antivirus

Modern versions of Windows come complete with a program called Windows Defender, which is primarily designed to counter spyware and pop-up advertisements on web pages. However, it is not intended to be a complete solution to problems with malicious software, and it should be used in addition to antivirus software rather than instead of it. If you do not wish to pay for a subscription to commercial antivirus software there are some good free alternatives available. One option is to use a free online virus checking facility to periodically scan your PC, but the drawback of this method is that there is no real-time protection for your PC. By the time you do a virus scan it is possible that a virus could have been spreading across your files for some time. By the time it is detected and removed it is likely that a significant amount of damage would already have been done.

Free antivirus

An antivirus program running on your PC will, like Windows Defender, provide real-time protection. In other words, it monitors disc drive activity, Internet activity, or anything that might involve a virus or other malicious program. If any suspicious files are detected, there is an attempt to alter system files, or any dubious activity is detected, the user is warned. In most cases the virus or other malicious program is blocked or removed from the system before it has a chance to do any harm.

The alternative to using online virus scanning is to download and install a free antivirus program. There are one or two totally free antivirus programs available on the Internet, where you do not even have to pay for any online updates to the database. The free version of AVG 9.0 from Grisoft is one that is certainly worth trying. The Grisoft site is at:

www.grisoft.com

On the home page there might be a link to the free version of the program, but it does not seem to feature quite as prominently in the home page as it did in the past. At the time of writing this, the web address for Grisoft's free software is:

http://free.avg.com/download-avg-anti-virus-free-edition

There is an instruction manual for the program in PDF format, and it is possible to read this online provided your PC has the Adobe Acrobat Reader program installed. However, it is definitely a good idea to download the manual and store it on the hard disc drive so that it is handy for future reference. It is a good idea to at least take a quick look

Fig.6.3 The main window of AVG Free gives access to various facilities

through the manual which, amongst other things, provides installation instructions. However, installation is fairly straightforward and follows along the normal lines for Windows software.

Background protection

AVG has a useful range of facilities and it is a very capable program. Like Windows Defender, it runs in the background and provides real-time protection, but you can also go into the main program. It can be launched via the normal routes, and by default there will be a quick-launch button near the bottom left-hand corner of the Windows Desktop. The program has various sections, and the initial window provides access to them (Figure 6.3). There is a facility here that manually updates the program's virus database, but the program will automatically update provided an active Internet link is available when the program is booted into Windows. In common with most antivirus programs you can set it to scan the system on a regular basis. A scan can also be started manually

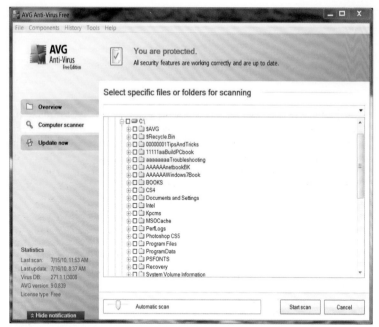

Fig.6.4 You can select the areas of the computer to be scanned

at any time, and the scan can cover the whole computer or selected areas (Figure 6.4).

Manual Removal

It is only fair to point out that an antivirus program can not automatically remove every type of computer infection. Most can be dealt with automatically, but some have to be removed manually. In such cases the program will usually provide removal instructions, or take you to a web site where detailed instructions can be found. Some of the steps required can be a bit technical, but everything should be fine provided you follow the instructions "to the letter". However, if you have a friend or relative who has a fair amount of computing expertise, enlisting their help is probably a good idea, for peace of mind if nothing else. Hopefully, the real-time protection will prevent any infection from taking hold in the first place.

Browsers

Size matters

Having been a user of the Internet since the early days, I have noticed an odd phenomenon whereby the size at which web pages are displayed has shrunk over the years. This is a strange occurrence, since the resolution used for web pages has actually increased somewhat over the years. The shrinking web page phenomenon is caused by improvements in monitor design. Modern monitors are much larger than those of ten or twenty years ago, and their maximum screen resolutions are higher. However, improvements in monitor technology have resulted in smaller pixels and more detailed pictures. With the monitors of twenty years or so ago the pixels were so large that you could often see the individual pixels, but this is something that even those with good eyesight are not likely to achieve these days. The shrinking pixels have to some extent been counteracted by web pages having higher resolutions, but web page designers like to make their pages easy to use for those having relatively simple computers such as small notebook and netbook PCs. This "lowest common denominator" approach means that many web pages are designed to work well with a screen width of 800 pixels, and

Fig.7.1 Most web pages are much narrower than the screen width

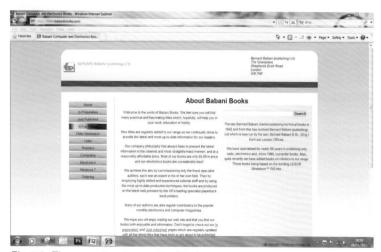

Fig.7.2 The page is a better fit with the zoom at 150 percent

there are still plenty that can display properly with a horizontal resolution of just 640 pixels.

The computer I am using to write this book has a horizontal screen resolution of 1680 pixels, which means that many web pages use less than half the screen width. The monitor I am using is a 23-inch type, but the displayed size of many web pages is commensurate with something more like an 11-inch monitor, making them difficult to read. There are ways around this problem, and one of them is to use the zoom or text size adjustment facility of the browser to increase the displayed size of pages. The zoom facility is the one that is most likely to obtain the desired effect, although it is probably worth trying the text size facility as well, and the two can be used together. In Internet Explorer they are both available from the view menu, and several preset sizes are available. Figure 7.1 shows a web page displayed at 100 percent, and in Figure 7.2 the zoom setting has been increased to 150 percent. Even at 150 percent the page does not come close to filling the screen from side to side, but it does make the page much easier to read. The 200 percent option made the page too wide to fit onto the screen properly.

Custom zoom

There is a custom option that, within reason, enables any desired zoom figure to be used. This makes it is possible to have a web page displayed at the full screen width (Figure 7.3), although it will take a little trial and

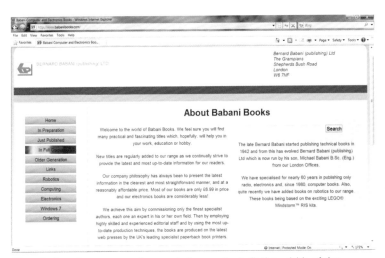

Fig.7.3 A web page can be made to precisely fit the width of the screen, but this is not necessarily a good idea

error to find the optimum zoom percentage. With a large monitor it is not always best to have pages filling the full width of the screen, or nearly doing so. The drawback of using the full screen width is that it results in relatively little coverage vertically. This increases the amount of scrolling required, and it can make some material difficult to use as only a fraction of it can be seen at one time. This can happen with diagrams and tables for example. The best zoom setting is the lowest one that enables the page to be read without difficulty.

Magnifier

At one time I had a gadget for making it easier to view awkward web pages, and I used to refer to it as my "hardware pan and zoom device". Everyone else referred to it as my magnifying glass! As I learned later, I was doing things the hard way, and there is no need for an external "hardware pan and zoom device" as there is a software equivalent built into Windows. It can be accessed from the Start menu by choosing All Programs, Accessories, Ease of Access, Magnifier. It has more than one mode of operation, and by default it enables the user to pan around a view of the screen that is zoomed by 200 percent. Perhaps of more use in the majority of situations, it has a Lens mode where a rectangular area around the cursor is magnified by a factor of two (Figure 7.4), giving the software version of a magnifying glass. Finally, there is the docked

Fig.7.4 The Magnifier accessory can give a magnified view of a rectangular area of the screen

mode (Figure 7.5), which uses a bar at the top of the screen to provide a zoomed view of the screen around the cursor. It is possible to adjust the height of the bar by dragging its lower edge, or the bar can be dragged to the bottom of the screen using anywhere within the bar as a handle. It can also be dragged to other parts of the screen, and it is then possible to adjust the size of the magnified area by dragging any of its edges.

Translation

Due to the international nature of the Internet it is likely that you will at least occasionally require a translation of some text, or perhaps even an entire web page. There are numerous free translation services available on the Internet, but when using them you have to bear in mind that they are based on a computer program that might not do a perfect job. Even an experienced human translator can make mistakes, so it would be unreasonable to expect an automated system to do so. Results with this type of service tend to be variable, with some text being translated quite accurately and with the original meaning intact. Other pieces of text become seriously scrambled, even when translated by a system that previously faired very well. To some extent the quality of a translation is dependent on the clarity of the original text. It is unreasonable to expect perfect prose from a piece of original text that is badly written, uses obscure slang terms and phrases, and contains spelling mistakes. There

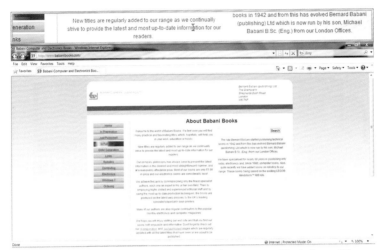

Fig.7.5   Here the top part of the screen gives a magnified view of the area around the cursor

can also be problems with words that have two or more meanings, leaving the translation software to best-guess at the correct meaning in each case. Some sites provide an automated translation service that is free, plus the option of using a human translator for a fee. Having someone translate text for you is unlikely to be cheap, but it might be worth the cost if it is important to have an accurate translation.

If you require (say) a translation from French to English, using any good search engine and a search string such as "French English translation" should produce some sites that provide the required service. FreeTranslation.com (Figure 7.6) is typical of an automatic translation site. Menus are used to select the source and output languages. The source text is either typed or pasted into the textbox on the left, and the translated text appears in the textbox on the right when the translate button is operated. A simple way of testing the accuracy of a translation engine is to get it to translate a couple of sentences into another language, and then get it to translate the translation back into English. With two sets of translation errors and approximations the text can become quite scrambled, but the meaning sometimes manages to survive quite well.

Web page translation

There are other types of translation facility available, and users of Google can install a translation toolbar that offers similar features to the free

Fig.7.6 FreeTranslation.com provides free translation services

online translation services. Sometimes you might need a web page translated, and there are translation services available that are designed specifically for this purpose. In fact some of the normal online translation facilities enable you to enter a URL, and the text on the specified page is then translated. Note that only proper text can be handled by automated web page translation services. Large and fancy text is often provided by graphics objects, and will be ignored by translation services. Some search engines provide the option of viewing normal or translated versions

Fig.7.7 There is a link for a translated version of the web page

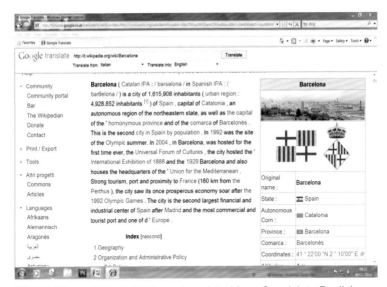

Fig.7.8 The web page has been translated from Spanish to English

of web pages. In Figure 7.7 for example, the Google search engine has provided a normal link for one of the listed sites, plus a "Translate this page" link. Operating the latter provides a version of the page that has been translated into English from the Spanish original (Figure 7.8). There is no choice of output language, and the text will be translated into the appropriate language for the Google site you are using. In this case it was Google.co.uk, and the text was therefore translated into English.

Nothing happens

Sometimes when using a web site it becomes apparent that something which is supposed to be happening is failing to make an appearance. There are several possible causes for things failing to make an appearance when using a web site, and in some cases it is simply that the web site has not been designed properly. Many sites have a facility that enables users to report problems, and it is a good idea to do so if you think that the problem is with the site rather than your computer. The site designer cannot fix a problem until he or she knows it exists. However, it is best to check out other possibilities rather than jumping to conclusions and immediately reporting a problem.

Reload

Probably the most common cause of problems is that the page has not downloaded properly. A browser should indicate when a page is downloading and when it has finished. Some facilities will probably work before a page has finished downloading, but it is likely that some will not, so wait until the page has completely downloaded before trying to use any clever facilities. The fact that a browser indicates it has finished downloading a page does not mean that it has actually managed to do so. Often it will be readily apparent that some items have not been downloaded, because there will be empty frames on the page where images or text should appear. In other cases it will be less obvious, but buttons will not work, operating links will have no effect, or something of this nature. Operating the reload button and trying again will often cure the problem. With Internet Explorer, and with some other browsers, operating the F5 key reloads the page, and using Control plus F5 reloads the page and the cache. This second option is useful if repeatedly reloading the page fails to make an improvement. The problem can be caused by errors in the cached data, and refreshing the cache should replace the erroneous data with a correct version of the page.

Wrong browser

Another potential cause of problems is that the web page you are trying to utilise is not compatible with the web browser in use. Most sites are compatible with Internet Explorer, but there can be problems with other browsers, particularly if you are not using one of the popular alternatives such as Firefox. Fortunately, Internet Explorer will still be available even if you switch to a different default browser, so the easy solution is to use Internet Explorer for any sites that are not compatible with your normal browser.

Missing add-ons

Problems with missing browser add-ons, or "plug-ins" as they are sometimes called, are quite common these days. The increasing sophistication of modern web sites results in an increasing number of them being reliant on users' computers being equipped with extra software, and without this software the web pages will not operate properly. The add-ons are small programs that are used to run the program code and data downloaded with the normal parts of web pages. These enable sound and video to be added to web pages, PDF documents to be displayed, and interactivity to be included. The common browser add-ons include Adobe Reader, Flash Player and Java. In some cases the web pages are still usable if the appropriate add-on is not installed on the user's computer, but results might not be usable in a worthwhile fashion. It is probably not worthwhile installing a range of common browser add-ons so that you are equipped for practically any eventuality. It is easier to simply install them as and when they are needed. The downloads are mostly quite small and can be installed quite quickly. With most sites that required an add-on of some kind you will get a warning message if the add-on is not detected, and there will often be the option of automatically installing that add-on. Failing that, there will probably be a link to a source for the add-on. As always with this type of thing, do not download and install a program unless you are sure that it is from a trustworthy source.

Other add-ons

It is worth checking to see if there are any good add-ons available for the web browser you are using. Here we are not talking in terms of add-ons that are required in order to use some web sites, but add-on facilities that make the browser better to use in some way. For example, there might be an add-on spelling checker. These mostly work in much the same way as the spelling checkers in word processors that check the text as you type it in. In the case of a browser's spelling checker, it checks the text as you type it into a textbox on a web page.

Ad-blockers

Ad-blockers are another popular type of browser add-on. These block many of the banner and pop-up advertisements that seem to feature on most web pages these days. This is not just a matter of getting rid of irksome advertisements. Most web pages will download significantly faster if the advertisements are blocked, and it reduces the amount of data downloaded during each surfing session. This second point is important if you have some form of capped Internet access. Exceeding the limit can be very expensive, especially with mobile broadband services, so a free ad-blocker could save a fair amount of money if you keep exceeding the cap.

Pop-up blockers

Ad-blockers should not be confused with the pop-up blockers that are available as add-ons, but are now an integral part of many browsers, including Internet Explorer. Pop-up blockers are designed to prevent most pop-up advertisements of the type that open in a new window. An ad-blocker is designed to block advertisements that are part of the web

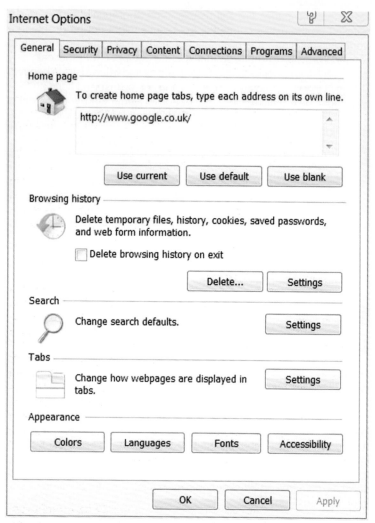

Fig.7.9 The General section of the Internet Options window

page being viewed. The two types are not mutually exclusive, and using both types should make surfing quicker and easier.

Browser privacy

Browsers normally store information about the sites you have visited during each surfing session, which is intended to be helpful rather than making it easy for anyone with access to your computer to spy on you. The stored data can make it easier to find a web page that was visited a few days earlier. Although you may have forgotten the web address, the browser will probably remember it perfectly. Browsers normally allow web sites to store small text files in a special folder on the hard disc drive. These files are called "cookies", and can have a variety of uses, some of which are helpful to the user while others are really just for the benefit of the web site owners. Allowing a web browser to store information about surfing sessions has its advantages, but many people are unhappy about any facility that effectively spies on them. Many users prefer not to have any of this information stored on computers that are used by others, and it is definitely not a good idea to allow it when using a computer to which there is public access.

Delete history

If you do not wish to have information about your surfing habits left on a computer it is important to use a browser that enables any stored information to be deleted easily. With Internet Explorer it is just a matter of going to the Tools menu and selecting Internet Options. The window that pops up will probably default to the General section (Figure 7.9) but if necessary you can display this section by operating the General tab near the top of the window. Operating the Delete button in the Browsing History section of the window results in all the information stored by the browser being deleted. If the checkbox is ticked, you can continue to surf the Internet and the files will be deleted when Internet Explorer is closed. It is possible to delete the browsing history files while leaving other files such as cookies intact. In order to do this it is just a matter of selecting Delete Browsing History from the tools menu.

InPrivate

Recent versions of Internet Explorer have a facility called InPrivate browsing that can be selected from the Tools menu. Selecting this option causes a new Internet Explorer window to be launched (Figure 7.10), and this can be used in the normal way, complete with multiple tabs. No browsing history is recorded for any of the tabs when using the new Internet Explorer window. The original Internet Explorer window operates normally, so make sure that you always use the right one when using the

Fig.7.10 Using the InPrivate mode launches a new browser window

InPrivate facility. It is not necessary to keep the original window open, so it is probably best to close it if you wish to use the InPrivate facility throughout the surfing session.

Its history

Of course, the reason that a browser stores your surfing history is to make it easy to return to a web page viewed earlier in a surfing session, or even one that was viewed several days earlier. With Internet Explorer this facility can be accessed by selecting History from the Favourites menu. A similar facility should be available from other browsers, and with Google's Chrome browser it can be accessed using the History entry in drop-down menu of the Tools button (the one that has the spanner icon).   This changes the main panel to look something like Figure 7.11, where a scrollable list of the sites visited over the last few days is provided. Left-clicking one of the links in the list will take you to the current version of that page.

Slowing down

At one time it seemed to be quite normal for a computer to steadily slow down over a period of time. This effect was often more pronounced

Fig.7.11 The History facility provides a list of recently visited sites

when surfing the Internet, with things at times practically grinding to a halt. It is less common these days, presumably due to the faster processors, higher capacity hard disc drives, and increased memory of modern computers. It can still happen though, especially when using an older computer or a modern portable PC of relatively low specification. The problem with an increasingly sluggish Internet is often the result of huge numbers of stored temporary files. These are intended to help speed things up, but after a while they often seem to have the opposite effect. Deleting the Internet history, as described previously, will often produce an improvement.

Windows Cleanup

Using the Windows Disk Cleanup facility to remove other unnecessary files from the hard disc drive might help to generally speed things up. This can be launched by going to the start menu and selecting All Programs, Accessories, System Tools, and Disk Cleanup. A small pop-

*Fig.7.12 You can select the types of file that will be deleted, or the
default selection can be used if preferred*

up window will appear if the computer is equipped with more than one
hard disc drive, and the drop-down menu is then used to select the
appropriate hard disc drive. It is normally drive C that needs to be
processed. After a delay while the disc is analysed, a new window will
appear (Figure 7.12). This lists various categories of file that have been
found. You can settle for the default settings, or go down the list yourself
and select the files that will be removed by ticking the appropriate
checkboxes. Operate the OK button to remove the selected files, and
confirm that you wish to delete the files when asked.

Finding things

The right result

In order to get anywhere when surfing the Internet you need to master web searching. As we will see shortly, getting lots of results from one of the popular search sites, or "search engines" as they are called, is quite easy. The difficult part is in getting a few high quality results. Getting two or three million matches is very impressive, but are you really going to search through that lot for what you need? Learn how to get a few quality results from a search engine and the worldwide web is your oyster. You will find what you need in minutes or even seconds instead of spending hours wading through thousands of results.

Search engines

A search engine is basically just a computer that contains details of the contents of a few billion web pages. Because the details are on the computer it is possible to search the pages very rapidly for the sort of information you require. On the downside, no search engine contains details of every web page. The search engines use automatic systems to scan the web for details of each site that is found. The contents of the Internet are constantly changing, so no matter how good a scanning system might be, its search engine will never be bang up to date. Also, the "snapshots" of the pages might have incomplete details of the information on some of the pages. Despite these minor limitations, search engines will usually find what you are looking for, if it is there. The basic function of a search engine is quite simple, and it starts with the user typing some words into a textbox. The search engine then looks through every web page stored in its database to find those that contain the word or words you have supplied. In most cases the default option is for pages that contain all the words to be selected, rather than pages that contain any one or more of them. It can be helpful to use less words in cases where a search produces few results or none at all, but the more usual problem is that there are vast numbers of pages that match your search terms.

Well chosen words

The key to success with web searches is to use the right words in the search string. Suppose that you are a keen golfer, and someone has told you that it has been scientifically proven that polishing your balls

Fig.8.1 An unlikely search string has produced over 89000 results

with royal jelly will make them go ten percent further. In order to check for confirmation on the web there is no point in using "golf" as the search word, since there are certainly millions of pages that contain this word. Using "golf" and "balls" is unlikely to reduce the count very much. Similarly, "royal" and "jelly" probably occur on a huge number of pages. On the other hand, using all four words should greatly reduce the number of matches. On the face of it, royal jelly and golf-balls have nothing in common, so any pages that contain both should have the scientific research we require.

Since I made up this amazing piece of research, one might reasonably expect these four words to produce no matches. In fact they produced over 89000 matches using the Google search engine (Figure 8.1). Why are there so many results for a totally bogus search? One reason is simply the huge number of web pages currently on the Internet. There are so many pages containing so many combinations of words that there is a reasonable chance of any string of a few words producing some matches. Try putting a few random words into a search engine and see what it turns up. I tried "plasma", "goose", "fire", and "fan", and Google responded with about 7650 pages containing these four seemingly unrelated words.

Useful quotations

One reason that there were so many matches in the bogus research example was that the words "royal" and "jelly" tended to occur separately on pages. With a normal search it does not matter whether the search words occur together or well apart. The engine is looking for the right words on the page and will find a match either way. Most search engines will place results higher in the list of results if the search words are close together, but this does not guarantee that the top results will all be relevant. Probably the most useful ploy for avoiding irrelevant results is to use quotation marks together with a short phrase. In this example royal jelly would be placed in double quotes ("royal jelly"), and a match would then be produced only if these two words occurred together and in the

Fig.8.2 Fewer matches, but still well over eleven thousand!

correct order. Figure 8.2 shows the result obtained using the modified search string. Incredibly, there are still over 11000 matching results!

Double double quotes

It is possible to reduce the number of matches still further, and adding more words into the search string might be a viable way of achieving this. Bear in mind though, that there are limits to the length of search strings. The search engine will ignore some of the search terms if you exceed the limits. Using two sets of quotation marks is often a more successful ploy. Placing "golf-balls" reduced the number of matches to just over a thousand matches, which is still a substantial number, but is a big improvement over the previous two versions of the search.

Punctuation

In the example search I used the totally separate words "golf" and "balls", but these two words are often hyphenated. Most search engines do not permit punctuation marks to be used in search strings, and will simply ignore them. Punctuation marks in web pages are usually treated as spaces. Therefore, as far as a search engine is concerned, there is no difference between "golf balls" and "golf-balls". On the other hand, neither of these will usually match with "golfballs". Mistakes are made in web pages, so you can sometimes get results using popular misspellings. These occur most frequently with the names of people and places (Davis instead of Davies for instance) and with the merging of hyphenated words.

Negative searching

There is another useful trick that can help to remove matches that are of no real use. Suppose that you are an amateur photographer interested in sites that give the results of lens tests. Using "lens" and "test" as the search string is likely starting point, but you might find that most of the sites suggested by the search engine have titles like "How to Test Your Camera Lens" and do not provide any lens tests. It is difficult to remove

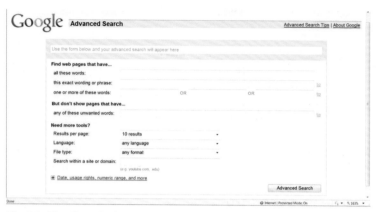

Fig.8.3 The Google Advanced search page

this type of site from the results by using more search words, since words in this type of site are likely to crop up in the sites of interest as well. The alternative method is to give the search program a word or words that can be used to eliminate pages from the results. In this case the word "how" could be used as the filter, with any page containing this word being removed from the list of matches.

A minus sign (-) or sometimes the word "NOT" is used in front of a word to indicate to the search engine that you are looking for pages that do not contain that word. Obviously this method does risk filtering out relevant pages that just happen to have the word you are avoiding. This method is especially risky with a general word such as "how", which can occur in just about any page about any subject. Anyway, if you can find a suitable word or words this is a method that will often provide good results.

Advanced search

When anything beyond a fairly basic search is required it is often easier to use the Advanced Search facility that is available from some search engines. The Google version is shown in Figure 8.3, and it is a form where the appropriate information is entered in the relevant fields. The textbox at the top provides an ordinary search, and pages must have all the words used here in order to match the search criteria. Below this is a textbox where a phrase can be entered, and a match will only be produced if an exact match for the phrase is found on a web page. In other words, this is the same as placing a phrase in double quotation

Fig.8.4 The two buttons give the otions of searching all web pages or only those in the UK

marks when using the standard version of the search engine. The textbox below this can be used to enter several words, and a match will be produced with web pages that have one or more of these words. The fourth textbox from the top can be used to prevent a match occurring with web pages that contain a specified word or words, and this is like using a minus sign or the word NOT in a normal search. Lower down the page there is a Language menu, and this can be used to block pages that are not in the selected language. Another menu enables a particular file type to be specified. For example, you can choose to search only PDF documents.

UK only

If you are only interested in UK sites and companies it is a good idea to go to the UK version of the search engine. Most of the large search companies have a general or US site with a .com address, plus other sites for specific countries. One of these is usually a UK web site having a .co.uk address. Alternatively, if you go to the .com address it is possible that the site will detect your country of origin and provide a page specifically for users in that country. The search engine will then tend to favour sites from within that country and demote matches from sites in other countries. With some search engines things can be taken a step further, and you opt to only search sites in your country. In the example of Figure 8.4 the Bing.com search engine has two radio buttons that

Fig.8.5 Yahoo! UK also has a facility for searching only UK web sites

enable all pages to be searched, or only those in the UK and Ireland. The UK version of the Yahoo site offers similar facilities (Figure 8.5). Two radio buttons enable the search to be restricted to the UK, or the whole of the Internet.

If you are looking for (say) a shop in the UK that sells lawnmower spare parts, by restricting the search to the UK it is possible to immediately filter out a vast number of sites that will be of no interest to you. The difference made by this type of filtering is usually vast. The number of matches will usually be reduced by well over 90 percent. These systems are less than perfect though. Apparently they operate by searching web servers located in the UK, but the nature of the Internet is such that UK sites can be hosted elsewhere in the world. Similarly, sites from elsewhere can be hosted in the UK. In practice this feature usually works quite well though.

Red-faced matches

Most search engines will happily track down whatever material is required, including pages that are pornographic or sexual in nature. Unfortunately, even quite innocent search strings can sometimes produce matches with sites that have a strong sexual content. When searching for web sites supporting the Flash graphics program I was not surprised that some of the matches were for sites having photographs of streakers in action. It was more surprising when a search for information on a graphics tablet called a Pen Partner produced a number of matches for pages giving details of a sex aid! This can all be a bit unfortunate if you are showing children or the vicar's wife how to search the Web, and the search for cheesecake recipes provides matches with some hardcore pornography sites.

However, it is a problem that is easily avoided, since most search engines have a facility that tries to filter out matches with pages that have a strong sexual content. In the case of Google it is a matter of using the Search Settings link near the top right-hand corner of the homepage, and then

Fig.8.6 Google's SafeSearch offers three levels of filtering

scrolling down to the settings for the SafeSearch filtering in the new page that appears (Figure 8.6). The current system defaults to moderate filtering, which does not actually filter very much. There are the alternative options of using strict filtering or no filtering at all.

Excessive filtering

It is only fair to point out that no adult filtering system can be guaranteed to be 100 percent effective, but a system of this type should filter the vast majority of potentially embarrassing search results and images. There is also a slight risk that this type of filtering will remove useful links. One method used by these systems is to look for "naughty" words in the scanned pages, and in some cases a page will be filtered if it contains a word that in turn contains a supposedly "naughty" word, even if the whole word is totally inoffensive. Some words can be "naughty" or inoffensive depending on the context. With a search for Mary Poppins you might find pages containing the name Dick Van Dyke were filtered out! However, the number of suitable matches removed by adult filtering is usually very small.

Categories

Many search engines now have the option of searching in a particular category, such as images, videos, shops and maps. Searching in a category can be a very good way of doing things as it will often filter vast numbers of irrelevant sites, and with a little luck it will get you straight to a suitable site or file. The search engine is used in the normal way when searching for a particular type of file

Fig.8.7 A Google image search

or web site, but the results might be displayed in a different fashion. Figure 8.7 shows the result of a search for images.

Maps

When maps are required, the maps section of a modern search engine is likely to provide the

Fig.8.8 The initial page when using the Maps facility of Google

required information in a fraction of the time it would take using a standard search engine. Switching to the Maps section of Google produces an initial large scale map (Figure 8.8). It is then a matter of entering one or more search terms in the usual way. This can be the name of a town or city, or something more specific such as a postcode or place within a town. Using the name of a road in double quotation marks plus the name of the town or city should result in the appropriate road being shown on a small scale map. For this example I used Colchester Castle Park Cricket as the search string, and Google Maps duly obliged with a

Fig.8.9 The location of the cricket ground has been found

map showing the exact location of this cricket ground (Figure 8.9). There are controls that enable the scale of the map to be altered, and panning can be achieved simply by dragging the map using the mouse. In Figure 8.10 I have changed to a larger scale and have panned the map northwards.

Fig.8.10   There are controls to alter the scaling of the map, which can also be panned using the mouse

Wildcards

Sometimes there can be search problems due to different spellings being used for the same thing or the same person. For example, names in Russian and many other languages are given their western spellings by converting them phonetically. In other words, the spelling is one that reflects the sound of the original name. The problem with this method is that the same name can be converted in two or more different ways, giving rise to alternative spellings for the same name. There can also be difficulties due to differences between American English and what for the lack of a better term we will call English English. Some search engines allow the use of wildcards, and these will often permit a single search to accommodate two different spellings. This feature is not as common as it used to be, but where allowed it permits the asterisk (*) to be used as a wildcard. A match will then be produced with any letter at that position in the word.

Missing pages

One of the most frustrating search problems is when you locate what looks like a very promising page using a search engine, but linking to that page produces some sort of error message rather than the page. You soon become familiar with the dreaded "404" error message which means that the page can not be found. There is a similar problem where the page appears, but it does not seem to have anything to do with the subject you are researching. When searching the Internet it is useful to bear in mind that it is copies of pages on a server that are being searched, and not the web itself. Web pages are deleted or altered from time to time, and this can produce discrepancies between the content of the database and the actual pages available on the Internet. An error message could indicate that the page has been deleted, or it could just be that the server has gone down. It could also be due to a problem on the route between your computer and the target web site. Try operating the browser's Refresh button, and repeat this once or twice if necessary. If the page still fails to load, make a note of the web address and try again later.

Where a page has been changed or deleted it might be possible to obtain some of the information it contained. In some cases it is possible to download the "snapshot" stored on the server, but bear in mind that this is usually an abbreviated version of the page. For most of the entries in a list of search results there is a Cached option. Selecting this option results in the snapshot of the page being displayed, rather than the current page being downloaded from the actual web site.

Blank results

As already pointed out, the usual problem when searching the Internet is too many matches rather than too few. You will not always find a plethora of matches though. This is something where you have to be realistic in your expectations. Although there is a massive amount of information available on the Internet, there is no guarantee that you will always be able to locate the information you require. The more obscure the subject, the lower the chances of success. If you draw a blank using one search engine, try another or even several more if necessary. I sometimes have to search for technical information about computing and electronics. It is quite normal for the first one, two or even three search engines to produce nothing useful, before I finally "come up trumps". As explained in the next section, there are ways of searching several sites simultaneously, and this approach is worthwhile if you are searching for something quite obscure and difficult to find.

A complete lack of response is often due to a spelling error. Remember that only an exact match will do when using double quotation marks. In a similar vein, if you are looking for pages that contain all the specified search words, a spelling error in one of the words will be sufficient to prevent any matches from being obtained. Particularly when dealing with names, double-check that you are spelling everything correctly. The same applies if you obtain numerous matches that are nothing to do with the subject matter you are seeking, or a lot of the sites are in a foreign language. The misspelled word might not mean anything in English, but it could be quite common in (say) German or Polish!

Shortcut

Many people make the mistake of using search engines when there is no real need to do so. If there is an obvious source of information always try that source first. For example, suppose you required some information on a Channel 4 program. You could use a search engine to find sites that cover that program, and you would probably find what you need before too long. On the other hand, you could simply go to the Channel 4 web site to look for information. There is a good chance of finding the information you require straight away, or failing that you may find a useful link to another site. Try the obvious sites first and only resort to a search engine if it is really necessary to do so.

Price comparison sites

In theory at any rate, the quick way to find the best price for just about anything is to use one of the numerous online price comparison sites. In practice matters are not that simple, and if you search for the best price on the same item using several price comparison sites it is quite likely that they will provide two or more different answers. It is possible that your own researches could find a better price than any of those listed by the comparison sites. There are several reasons for these inconsistencies, such as some sites updating their data more frequently than others, and the number of retailers checked being different for each site. Many of these sites receive payments from the retailers for directing buyers to their sites, and they only check sites where a deal has been done between themselves and retailers. A comparison site that checks a large number of sources is more likely to find the best price than one which only checks a few. A site that updates its results very frequently will not necessarily be any better at finding the best price, but it will be less prone to directing users to great offers that expired last week.

Vouchers

If you are going to use price comparison sites it is best to try several of them and compare the results. This to some extent negates the point of using a price comparison service, which is to avoid checking several sites. However, it requires only a little extra time and effort, and there is a good chance that the best price on offer is genuinely the best price, or something very close to it. An advantage of using price comparison sites is that they sometimes have voucher codes that can be used to obtain a discount. Obviously the voucher needs to apply to a price that is already very good if it is to produce a genuinely worthwhile deal, but it is sometimes possible to make substantial savings in this way. I recently obtained a twenty percent discount on a mobile broadband contract, which was a saving of over fifty pounds over duration of the contract.

Reviews

If you enter the word "review" and the name of a product into a search engine, in amongst the usual shops and comparison sites you will probably get links to a few sites that have good reviews of the item. There are two main types of review, which are the professional and user varieties. The professional reviews are probably the best place to start, as these will be written by people who are familiar with the type of product being tested, and they will know how it compares to other products of the same type. Many of these reviews are long and detailed, and should let you know exactly what you are buying. Some of the user reviews are very well written and helpful, but many seem to be produced by people who lack a proper understanding of the product. Also, bear in mind that people that have problems with products are more likely to write a review than those who find the product satisfactory or very good. It is still worth reading some user reviews. It is likely that a product is flawed if the same problem keeps cropping up in review after review.

Safety first

It is important to take due care when buying online. It is best to avoid new sites that offer popular goods at very low prices. Many bogus sites of this type appear and rapidly disappear, especially in the lead up to Christmas. Do not assume that a site is legitimate just because it has a very professional looking web site. It is much safer to deal with established sites that have a good "track record". Some of the price comparison sites have user reviews of online traders, and an established online retailer should have received a substantial number of reviews over the course of a few years. Watch out for online sellers that give the impression of being based in the UK when they are actually based outside the UK, and probably outside the EU as well. The fact that a company has a .co.uk web address and a UK phone number does not guarantee that it is a UK company. It is not necessarily a mistake to deal with a company based outside the UK or the EU, but there are potential disadvantages, such manufacturers' guarantees that will not be honoured in the UK, goods that differ from the UK specification, and consumer rights that fall short of EU standards. Paying by credit card is generally considered the best method for items costing over one hundred pounds. You might then be able to make a claim to the credit card company if things go badly wrong. Check the cost of postage and packing before placing an order, and remember to take it into account when comparing prices.